Ideology: A Very Short Introduction

Very Short Introductions available now:

Michael Freeden

IDEOLOGY

A Very Short Introduction

OXFORD
UNIVERSITY PRESS

OXFORD
UNIVERSITY PRESS

Great Clarendon Street, Oxford OX2 6DP

Oxford University Press is a department of the University of Oxford.
It furthers the University's objective of excellence in research, scholarship,
and education by publishing worldwide in

Oxford New York

Auckland Bangkok Buenos Aires Cape Town Chennai
Dar es Salaam Delhi Hong Kong Istanbul Karachi Kolkata
Kuala Lumpur Madrid Melbourne Mexico City Mumbai Nairobi
São Paulo Shanghai Taipei Tokyo Toronto

Oxford is a registered trade mark of Oxford University Press
in the UK and in certain other countries

Published in the United States
by Oxford University Press Inc., New York

© Michael Freeden 2003

British Library Cataloguing in Publication Data

Data available

Library of Congress Cataloging in Publication Data

Data available

ISBN 978-0-19-280281-1

13 15 17 19 20 18 16 14

Typeset by RefineCatch Ltd, Bungay, Suffolk
Printed in Great Britain by
Ashford Colour Press Ltd, Gosport, Hampshire

Contents

List of illustrations

Chapter 1
Should ideologies be ill-reputed?

Ideology is a word that evokes strong emotional responses. On one occasion, after I had finished a lecture that emphasized the ubiquity of political ideologies, a man at the back of the audience got up, raised himself to his full height and, in a mixture of affrontedness and disdain, said: 'Are you suggesting, Sir, that I am an ideologist?' When people hear the word 'ideology', they often associate it with 'isms' such as communism, fascism, or anarchism. All these words do denote ideologies, but a note of caution must be sounded. An 'ism' is a slightly familiar, faintly derogatory term – in the United States even 'liberalism' is tainted with that brush. It suggests that artificially constructed sets of ideas, somewhat removed from everyday life, are manipulated by the powers that be – and the powers that want to be. They attempt to control the world of politics and to force us into a rut of doctrinaire thinking and conduct. But not every 'ism' is an ideology (consider 'optimism' or 'witticism'), and not every ideology is dropped from a great height on an unwilling society, crushing its actually held views and convictions and used as a weapon against non-believers. The response I shall give my perplexed man at the back in the course of this short book is the one put by Molière in the mouth of M. Jourdain, who discovered to his delight that he had been speaking prose all his life. We produce, disseminate, and consume ideologies all our lives, whether we are aware of it or not. So, yes, we are all ideologists in that we have understandings of the political environment of which we are part, and have views about the merits and failings of that environment.

Imagine yourself walking in a city. Upon turning the corner you confront a large group of people acting excitedly, waving banners and shouting slogans, surrounded by uniformed men trying to contain the movement of the group. Someone talks through a microphone and the crowd cheers. Your immediate reaction is to decode that situation quickly. Should you flee or join, or should you perhaps ignore it? The problem lies in the decoding. Fortunately, most of us, consciously or not, possess a map that locates the event we are observing and interprets it for us. If you are an anarchist, the map might say: 'Here is a spontaneous expression of popular will, an example of the direct action we need to take in order to wrest the control of the political away from elites that oppress and dictate. Power must be located in the people; governments act in their own interests that are contrary to the people's will.' If you are a conservative, the map may say: 'Here is a potentially dangerous event. A collection of individuals are about to engage in violence in order to attain aims that they have failed, or would fail, to achieve through the political process. This illegitimate and illegal conduct must be contained by a strong police grip on the situation. They need to be dispersed and, if aggressive, arrested and brought to account.' And if you are a liberal, it may say: 'Well-done! We should be proud of ourselves. This is a perfect illustration of the pluralist and open nature of our society. We appreciate the importance of dissent; in fact, we encourage it through instances of free speech and free association such as the demonstration we are witnessing.'

Ideologies, as we shall see, map the political and social worlds for us. We simply cannot do without them because we cannot act without making sense of the worlds we inhabit. Making sense, let it be said, does not always mean making good or right sense. But ideologies will often contain a lot of common sense. At any rate, political facts never speak for themselves. Through our diverse ideologies, we provide competing interpretations of what the facts

"Congratulations! What got you here is your total lack of commitment to any ideology."

1. A reward or an ironic comment?

might mean. Every interpretation, each ideology, is one such instance of imposing a pattern – some form of structure or organization – on how we read (and misread) political facts, events, occurrences, actions, on how we see images and hear voices. Ideological maps do not represent an objective, external reality. The patterns we impose, or adopt from others, do not have to be sophisticated, but without a pattern we remain clueless and uncomprehending, on the receiving end of ostensibly random bits of information without rhyme or reason.

Why, then, is there so much suspicion and distrust of ideologies? Why are they considered to be at the very least alien caricatures, if not oppressive ideational straitjackets, that need to be debunked and dismantled to protect a society against brainwashing and dreaming false dreams? There has rarely been a word in political language that has attracted such misunderstanding and opprobrium. We need to clear away some debris in order to appreciate that, to the contrary, there are very few words that refer to such an important and central feature of political life.

3

In discussing ideologies, this book will mainly refer to political ideologies and will argue that ideologies are political devices. When ideology is used in other senses – such as the ideology of the impressionists or of Jane Austen – the word is borrowed or generalized to indicate the much vaguer notion of the cultural ideas guiding the field or steering the practitioner in question. One problem with the term 'ideology' is that too many of its users have shied away from injecting it with a reasonably precise, useful, and illuminating meaning.

The initial coiner of the term 'ideology', Antoine Destutt de Tracy, writing in the aftermath of the French Revolution, intended to create a proper branch of study concerned with ideas. He sought to establish ideals of thought and action on an empirically verifiable basis, from which both the criticism of ideas and a science of ideas would emerge. That enterprise was very much in line with the positivist movement in 19th-century France, which held out the

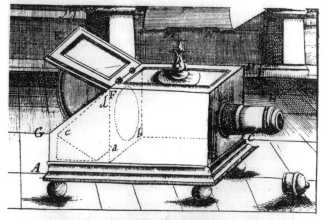

THE HISTORY OF THE CAMERA OBSCURA

5. *Johann Zahn. Reflex box camera obscura, 1685*

2. **A camera obscura.**

possibility of studying society with the precise tools characteristic of a natural science. Our post-positivist age does not accept that the range of human thought and imagination can be given the accuracy and permanence that these earlier codifiers of knowledge had anticipated. But one residue needs to be taken seriously. Destutt de Tracy's intentions reflect the need that current scholars perceive for a professional and dedicated approach to the study of ideology. Having, then, paid homage to the originator of the word, and acknowledging the task ahead, we first proceed to the early and still influential developers of the product, Karl Marx and Friedrich Engels, who took a very different line.

The Marxist takeover

In *The German Ideology*, Marx and Engels reacted to the prevailing German cultural and philosophical fashions they had experienced. The spiritual and romantic nature of German idealist thought, they contended, was fuelled by erroneous conceptions. One of these attributed independent existence to ideas, thought, and consciousness when attempting to exchange illusory thought for correct thought. But in so doing, argued Marx and Engels, German philosophers merely fought against phrases rather than coming to terms with the real world. Philosophy thus concealed reality, and adopted the form of what Marx and Engels called an ideology. They maintained that 'in all ideology men and their circumstances appear upside-down as in a camera obscura'. By that analogy they meant that ideology was an inverted mirror-image of the material world, further distorted by the fact that the material world was itself subject to dehumanizing social relations under capitalism. The role of ideology was to smooth over those contradictions by making them appear as necessary, normal, and congruous. That way social unity could be maintained and enhanced. Ideology was a sublimation – in its various guises such as morality, religion, and metaphysics – of material life. In addition, ideology was disseminated by those who specialized in the mental activity of sublimation: priests offering 'salvation' were an early example of that 'emancipation' from the real world. That dissemination could be an act of deliberate manipulation, but it could also – especially for Engels – be an unconscious, or self-deceptive, process. Ideology was one manifestation of the pernicious effects of the division of labour. In this case, the division of labour caused human thought to be abstracted from the material world, producing instead pure theory, or ethics, or philosophy.

Marx and Engels added to that view of ideology a further dimension, which was to be highly influential. They associated ideology and class, asserting that the ideas of the ruling class were the ruling ideas. Ideological illusions were an instrument in the hands of the rulers, through the state, and were employed to exercise control and domination; indeed, to 'manufacture history' according to their interests. Moreover, the filtering of interests through a container – ideology – permitted them, and ideology itself, to be represented as if they were truth-claims that possessed universal, rational validity. That representation assisted the wielders of ideology in forging the myth of a unified political community, through illusory laws, cultural direction, and 'verbal masquerading' – that is, the power over language.

The controllers of human conduct and thought even convinced the members of the subservient class – the proletariat – that the dominant bourgeois ideology was theirs as well. An exploited worker actually believed that it was a good idea to get up in the morning and work 14 hours for a pittance in her employer's factory, because she had internalized the ideological view that such dehumanizing work was an inevitable part of the industrial order, that it was a free act on her part, that markets gave everyone an equal chance, and that earning one's keep by renting out one's labour to others was central to one's sense of dignity. Ideology thus concentrated on external appearances, not on a real understanding of what was essential. The abnormal became normal through ideological sleight of hand and through fetishizing (bestowing a sacred and mystifying status on) commodities and the markets in which they circulated; for example, people worshipped money rather than respecting the genuine productive processes that generated wealth. Here – a tendency evident in his later work, especially *Capital* – Marx focused on the actual capitalist practices from which ideology emanated, rather than on the distorted ideas of philosophers and ideologists. Understandably, a major mission of what later became known as Marxism was to unmask and demystify the dissimulative nature of ideology. The critical exposition of ideology would expose the false aspirations of its promoters, and install instead a set of wholesome social practices that provided the empirical basis of true social consciousness.

We can see a rather persuasive picture of ideology emerging from the Marxist approach. Ideology was the product of a number of basic, if unhealthy, causes. One was the need for simplified and easily marketable accounts of the world around us. A second was the desire of some individuals and groups for power and control over others. A third was a growing tendency to break up human activity into separate compartments – the division of labour – and to alienate thought and action from each other. Ideology reinforced all that, and it kept societies in a state of ignorance and suffering. One might justifiably conclude that Marxism accorded ideas considerable power, and so it did – to ideas that appeared in the form of ideology. But for Marx such concentrated power was wrong, as it blocked the possibility of human emancipation. All these features appear in a much more sophisticated manner in Marx's own writings, but it is broadly in these forms that they have been subsequently replicated in vulgarized yet influential views of ideology.

Before lining up to praise or blame the Marxist theory of ideology, we need to ask ourselves: what has to hold for those arguments to make sense? First, they depend on the crucial distinction between true consciousness and distorted or false beliefs. In order to claim that our understanding of the (political) world is based on an illusion, we must be confident that non-illusory knowledge is attainable. Marx believed that truth would emerge once distortion was removed; in other words, that true human and material relations were both a default position that was obscured by social and ideological distortions and a scientifically anticipated outcome of future social development. That truth could be conclusively excavated (it was certainly not discovered through revelation or intuition, in which Marx didn't believe) was a non-negotiable assumption. For that very reason, as we shall see, Marx's critics labelled this fundamental assertion itself an ideological belief, thus turning the tables on Marx. But the existence of social truths may not be as obvious as it seems. Some factual knowledge may appear to be evident – 'I am looking at a group of people engaged in a protest meeting' – but, as we have seen, *what* we come away knowing about that group will differ according to the interpretative map we use. There is a well-known phrase: 'let's judge the case on its merits'. But cases aren't equipped with merits that jump out at us; we impose merits *on* the case, in line with the beliefs and values to which we already subscribe.

Second, and consequently, those arguments depend on the ephemeral nature of ideology. If ideology is a distortion, it will disappear once true social relations have been (re)introduced. If it is the product of an unnatural and alienating division between the material and the spiritual, it will disappear once the material roots of the spiritual are recognized. And if it consolidates a power relationship between ruling and ruled classes, it will disappear once such power relationships are transformed into a democratic sense of social community and equality. So ideology is dispensable; it is a pathological product of historical circumstances and it will wither away when they improve.

Third, the Marxist conception of ideology has contributed to a unitary understanding of ideology. If ideology is indeed an unfortunate smokescreen that covers up reality, the faster we dispose of it the better. In particular, there is no point in examining it for what it is, nor in distinguishing among different variants of ideology. For many Marxists, though not for all, as we shall see, ideology is part of a 'superstructure' that has no intrinsic value. As a result, their approach to ideology has discouraged any interest in the nature and permutations of the concealing smokescreen. Marx's quasi-messianic conviction that a socialist, undistorted society would prevail meant that present defects were worth deploring, not exploring. It is as if a student of political institutions decided that it was a waste of time to study the House of Commons because its debates exhibit inferior political practice: they display loutish behaviour, competitive antagonism, gross inefficiencies, and ridiculous seating arrangements. Instead, declares the scholar, let's devote our intellectual efforts to predicting the development of a best-practice legislature, which can be defended and endorsed permanently.

In order to claim that political practices or ideas are distorted, we have to be certain that they possess undistorted forms. But even if we are convinced of the current ubiquity of such distortions, a student of politics could persuasively contend that these are interesting social phenomena, and they require analysis if we are to understand the nature of the political in existing societies. Once we plunge into the smokescreen, into the substance of ideology, we will find both commonalities and variations: a complex and rich world that awaits discovery. In short, a large number of concrete ideologies inhabit Marx's abstract category of 'ideology', and their shared features provide immensely significant aids to making sense of the political world.

Fourth, another facet of the unitary character of Marxist ideology is that ideologies are part of a single, even total, account of the political world. They are the linchpin that holds together a seamless view of the world, papering over its internal contradictions. This image of coordinated totality prevailed for a long time in portrayals of ideology, contributing to its inclusive nature and to an insistence by some ideologists that they were infallible. We need however to be convinced that such monolithic views of the world not only exist, but have persuasive force. In the absence of such persuasive force, physical coercion has all too often become necessary to hold ideology in place.

Fifth, the role of ideologists has been exaggerated. Although Marxist logic points to the social provenance of ideology, its source has frequently turned out to be much smaller than an entire class. The Marxist linking of ideology to power relations as well as to the manipulation of the masses has often resulted in the identification of a professional group of ideologues, and even in the detection of the impact of single individuals. For some scholars, ideologues are intellectuals with a dangerous sense of mission – namely, to change the world according to a specific absolute vision. This perspective entails a rather hierarchical view of the world. It also suggests that both the production and the dissemination of intellectual goods constitute a monopoly. The Marxist theory of class assists in supporting such views, though the intellectuals that figure in those theories sometimes act independently, less determined by their own material bases than Marxists assume. The association of ideology with such intellectuals has also contributed to the commonly held view that ideologies are a priori, abstract, and non-empirical. That view is widely believed by current politicians, by the press, and by quite a few scholars as well, especially in the Anglophone world, with its own myth of empiricism, and in the German-speaking world, still under the influence of the vocabulary employed by its countryman, Marx.

What, then, is still of value in the Marxist emphasis on unmasking ideology? Four things, perhaps. First, we have picked up from Marx the significance of social and historical circumstances in moulding political (and other) ideas. We accept as a truism that people are importantly the product of their environment, though there is still much debate on the relative weight of the environmental, the genetic, and the individual capacity for choice. Relieved of some of the Marxist baggage, ideas and ideologies are understood as the product of groups. They are also part of the cultural milieu that shapes, and is shaped by, our activities.

Second, ideas matter. Marx may have seen the current domain of ideology as a harmful illusion, but even in that sphere the implication is that ideas are not merely rhetorical. If ideas appear not only as truths but in such commanding guises as an ideology, they need to be taken very seriously indeed, and accorded an even more central role than Marx himself had done.

Third, ideologies are endowed with crucial political functions. They order the social world, direct it towards certain activities, and legitimate or delegitimate its practices. Ideologies exercise power, at the very least by creating a framework within which decisions can be taken and make sense. That power doesn't have to be exploitative or dehumanizing, but then only some anarchists would argue that power – even as an enabling phenomenon – can be dispensed with completely.

Fourth, the Marxist method has bequeathed something of importance even to non-Marxists. It is, simply, that what you see is not always what you get. If we wish to understand ideologies, we have to accept that they contain levels of meaning that are hidden from their consumers and, frequently, from their producers as well. The study of ideology therefore encompasses in large part – though certainly not entirely – the enterprise of decoding, of identifying structures, contexts, and motives that are not readily visible.

Chapter 2
Overcoming illusions: how ideologies came to stay

The story of the emergence of the concept of ideology from under the Marxist wing is a complex one that still hasn't reached its conclusion. But we can identify three 20th-century individuals – Karl Mannheim, Antonio Gramsci, and Louis Althusser – whose contributions to the range of meanings that the notion of ideology carried were of major consequence. It is true, also, that the study of ideology has made further strides since those three thinkers refocused our understanding. But perhaps the most significant outcome of their interventions – each in their own singular way operating from Marxist premises – was that they transformed our conception of ideology from the transient epiphenomenon Marx and Engels had made it out to be into a permanent feature of the political and opened the way to removing some of its pejorative connotations.

The social roots of ideology: Karl Mannheim

The intellectual achievement of Karl Mannheim, the sociologist and social philosopher (1893–1947), was to extract from the Marxist approach a key insight: ideology was a reflection of *all* historical and social environments. While Marx condemned the social conditions under capitalism as the source of ideological illusion, Mannheim realized that it was a feature of any social environment to influence the thought processes of human beings and, moreover, that knowledge was 'a co-operative process of group life'. In those acute senses, ideology was not a passing chimera. Moreover, the first indications of analytical pluralism entered the fray: societies had many different social groups and class environments; therefore, such 'multiplicity of ways of thinking' could produce more than one ideology. This pluralist potential of ideologies became highly significant in later theories of ideology, as we shall see. In laying the groundwork for the scholarly study of ideology, Mannheim implicitly resurrected the agenda of Destutt de Tracy that Marx and Engels had largely ignored.

For Mannheim, ideology had both social and psychological manifestations. Ideology was not only employed to manipulate deliberately those under its control. He also emphasized the unconscious presuppositions that guided human thinking, as well as the irrational foundations of knowledge. After all, social groups operate on the basis of shared rituals, prejudices, stories, and histories – elements that ideologies incorporate. For most of us it is quite difficult to see ourselves from a different perspective and note the customs and habits that we internalize unthinkingly and uncritically. The unconscious and the irrational could only be unmasked at a more advanced stage of social development, when attempts would be made to justify them rationally. The effectiveness of that unmasking was often limited, for Mannheim began by adopting the Marxist view of ideology as the obscuring of the real condition of society by the interests of a ruling class. But to this static view of ideology he added the parallel notion of utopia. Utopia was a vision of a future or perfect society held by oppressed groups who, bent on changing and destroying existing society, saw only its negative aspects and were blind to the situation as it really was. We may quibble about that distinction. What Mannheim termed utopia we would now call a progressive or transformative ideology, as distinct from a traditional or conservative one. That aside, Mannheim held that new explanatory theories, spread by analysts such as himself, would enlighten the less aware producers and consumers of ideology, who were much too caught up in its web.

The psychological features of ideology were for Mannheim, as for Marx, conscious distortions, calculated lies, or forms of self-deception. This was the particular conception of ideology. Mannheim related it to specific arguments, more or less deliberately misrepresented by individuals. But the total conception of ideology was a *Weltanschauung*, an all-encompassing view of the world adopted by a given group, always reflecting the general ideas and thought-systems of an historical epoch. Here was a dual challenge: first, to the Marxist blindness to competing ideological systems that emerged from different modes of existence; and second, to the political philosopher's search for universal and timeless truths about the social life and conduct of individuals. In acknowledging the holistic nature of the total conception of ideology, Mannheim was working his way towards understanding it in an ordered and systemic way. An ideology was an interdependent structure of thinking, typical of social systems, that could not be reduced to the aggregated and psychologically comprehensible views of concrete individuals.

Mannheim also alighted on an issue that still divides students of ideology. Marxists, as we have seen, defied the populist implications of their own logic by singling out the abstracted and alienated fabricators of false knowledge, the philosophers and priests. But a total conception of ideology indicated the broad origins of ideology in group and even mass attitudes and views. This, Mannheim believed, was a gradual process. An intelligentsia was a group 'whose special task it is to provide an interpretation of the world' for their society. As societies evolved and social mobility increased, the members of an intelligentsia began to be recruited from a more varied social background. They were no longer associated with a determinate and closed body. Nevertheless, the intelligentsia were still allotted a special role in Mannheim's scheme of things. They provided an increasingly independent, non-subjective, interpretation of the world. For Mannheim, an intellectual was not necessarily a person of education or culture, but one who could detach her- or himself from their conditioning social background and 'free-float' among the different social and historical perspectives available in their society.

Here, though, Mannheim revealed his Marxist-inspired roots, for he believed in the possibility of a unified sociology of knowledge, produced by these free-floaters, and transcending the partial viewpoints of ideology and utopia alike - a reversion to the possibility of social truths. The key to this process lay in Mannheim's distinction between relativism and relationism. Relativism was the recognition that all thought was linked to the concrete, historical situation of the thinker and that it had no objective, universal, standing. But it led to an unwelcome reaction: if that was true, all thought could be dismissed as subjective. In that case oppressors and warmongers could know no better: they were merely the products of their environments. That, obviously, was an unreliable method of assessing social motives and action, and Mannheim replaced it with relationism. Relationism, like relativism, acknowledged the contextual location of thought and the absence of absolute truth in social and historical matters – even Marxism itself, that ostensible anti-ideology, was exposed by Mannheim as an ideology. Some now refer to this problem as 'Mannheim's paradox', namely, that we cannot expose a viewpoint as ideological without ourselves adopting an ideological viewpoint.

But relationism mooted three things. First, it affirmed that ideas were only comprehensible if we appreciated their mutual interdependence. It was impossible to understand one element of thought without ascertaining its relation to other, sustaining, and interacting ideas. Second, that holistic framework offered the possibility of a social standpoint from which different relationist understandings are assessed, and from which 'truths' and knowledge of the real world could be extracted. This enabled the analyst to distinguish among the quality of different ideological arguments. It was possible to explore diverse ideas circulating in a society, to weigh them up one against the other, and to decide what

3. Karl Mannheim.

features of those ideas might both be valid and mutually supportive. Mannheim was unclear on whether these historically extracted truths had a more permanent life. But, third, it was only with the development of the total conception of ideology that the *sociology* of knowledge could surface. That allowed the term ideology to shift in its meaning from being 'simply' designated as a means of exercising, or resisting, political domination to being a critical analytical tool that made sense of ideological arguments themselves. The question was no longer merely what ideology *did*, but what kind of thinking ideology *was*. Mannheim's contribution lay not only in recognizing the importance of the latter question. He re-tuned the former question so that it forsook its negative resonance in favour of an engagement with the positive functions of ideology as well.

The outcome of Mannheim's approach was to be a 'science of politics' and it was in surveying and assessing the partial truths of a society that the intelligentsia found its mission. In identifying the inherent limitations of existing relativist views, Mannheim thought to take an important stride in the direction of value-free knowledge, though he was loath to take any final step towards absolute and conclusive knowledge. Ideologies, he observed, were always changing and dynamic, and so was knowledge. Yet the positivist streak that began with Destutt de Tracy and had worked its way through Marx and Engels was retained. Ideas could be studied objectively; more significantly, they could be *generated* objectively – as knowledge of social reality. Although Mannheim had detected, through his notion of relativism, an irreconcilable plurality of political ideas, he did not regard that pluralism in itself as a rich resource for social life. If each of the plural viewpoints was held absolutely by its proponents, they could be destabilizing factors that had to be overcome.

The shortcomings of Mannheim's approach are evident. He believed that a group of individuals capable of rising above their class and historical context would break the hold of the ideologies emanating from that context. He assumed that the intelligentsia would all arrive at a single point of agreement, and that such a point would be non-ideological. We now tend to be more sceptical of the possibility of scholarly consensus. We accept that for many social and historical issues there may be more than one convincing explanation or interpretation, and that scholars cannot entirely rid themselves of their values and preferences. Mannheim clearly wanted to avoid a situation in which all ideological positions assert their exclusive worth, and he anticipated instead 'a new type of objectivity'. But there was no need to drop ideology, for holding on to some form of relativism does not lead to the condoning of all viewpoints as *equally* valuable.

We might put this as follows. The objectivist claims that only one road leads to Rome. The extreme relativist claims that all roads lead to Rome (though they may lead elsewhere as well), and that we cannot know whether one route is better than another – it's entirely up to the traveller's opinion. The sensible constrained relativist claims that many, but far from all, roads lead to Rome, and that they vary in quality, speed, and safety. Different routes may be recommended depending on which of the road's attributes the traveller values most, but the appraisal of these attributes is based on comparing the traveller's private judgement with accepted standards of assessing road surfaces, traffic density, distance, and construction. At most, Mannheim could have talked of a form of intersubjectivity, that is, overlapping but still relativist understandings.

We might also query the capacity of individuals to rid themselves so neatly of their ideologies (and shall do so in Chapter 3). Mannheim's approach foreshadowed some of the 'end of ideology' debates of the mid-20th century. They maintained that modern societies were converging on agreed principles and policies, such as the welfare state or the consumer society. Consequently fundamental divergences of opinion would disappear. That overlooked the fact that, even when all agree on a viewpoint, you still end up with *one* ideology rather than none. We still need *a* map.

Finally, there remains the question of the critical role of ideology. For Marx, the very notion of ideology served the one critical purpose of alerting us to its insidious nature and the need to unmask it. Mannheim appears to vacillate between that approach and the acknowledgement that ideology is a worthwhile object of study. He both wished to distil the approximate truths from within contending ideologies and to explore their varied forms. He recognized the ephemeral and dynamically unfolding nature of human thought, but also the permanence of some of its regularities that could reveal human destiny. This was sociology with a normative twist, in which the scholar would ultimately value certain historical developments and certain ideologies more than others, and do so through understanding the totality of history. That constitutes a comprehensive view, but not a final one. Rather it is a 'relative optimum' for our time and our place.

Mannheim's subtlety of approach puts him in the very forefront of theorists of ideology, but he was still suspended in a no man's land between old and new understandings. He undoubtedly left to posterity a cardinal imperative for political theory: it needed to be made aware of its own assumptions and categories. A naive view of thinking about politics – one that saw it as a pure form, elevated above the contingencies and imperfections of everyday life – would no longer be possible. In order to understand political thought, much of it had to be approached and deciphered as ideology, as a product of historical and social circumstances. Marx had applied the critical kernel of his notion of ideology to eliminating its distortions of reality. Mannheim applied the critical kernel of his notion of ideology to highlighting the impermanent and malleable nature of all human thought. Whether that impermanence was the consequence of a special historical context or itself a permanent feature of ideology was a question Mannheim left open for others to address. But he kept one vital issue, that bedevilled even later Marxists, hovering in the air: is it possible, and is it useful, to detach ideology from the Marxist notion of class?

The spread of ideology: Antonio Gramsci

The contribution of Antonio Gramsci, the radical Italian Marxist theorist and activist (1891–1937) to the analysis of ideology is significant in ways both different from and parallel to Mannheim's. Gramsci modified the Marxist understanding of the term working *within* a broadly Marxist tradition. He is best-known to students of ideology for his notion of hegemony. Ideological hegemony could be exercised by a dominant class, the bourgeoisie, not only through exerting state force but through various cultural means. Gramsci shifted ideology away from being solely a tool of the state. Ideology operated and was produced in civil society, the sphere of non-state individual and group activity. Here again the intellectuals surfaced as the major formulators and conductors of ideology and as non-governmental leaders wielding cultural authority. Their permeation of social life was characteristically based on the manufacturing of consent among the population at large, so that the masses would regard their own assent as spontaneous. That process of forming consent – which Gramsci termed leadership as distinct from domination – necessarily preceded, and paved the way for, the dominance wielded through governmental power. Gramsci was therefore inclined to sharpen the distinction between ideology as a more conscious creation for its producers, and a more unconscious one for its consumers.

One perspicacious move forward of Gramsci's in investigating ideological hegemony was his sensitivity to its importance, albeit from a Marxist perspective. The establishment of hegemony involved the coordination of different interests and their ideological expressions, so that an all-embracing group, possibly society as a whole, would be engaged. Hegemony produced compromise – an equilibrium that took some account of the subordinate groups. Marxist class confrontation gave way to the building up of solidarity in a manner that could serve the Marxist end of a unified community. That was so because different ideologies maintained a state of conflict until one of them, or a combination of some, prevailed. The result was an intellectual, moral, economic, and political unity of aims with the semblance of universality. But there was also a liberal undertone to Gramsci's theory of ideology, which he himself did not emphasize. It was based on a voluntarism embedded in civil society that we associate – at least on the surface – with free choice, consent, and material or intellectual markets. Another chink had been opened in the Marxist armour.

Gramsci saw the notion of hegemony as a great advance, both philosophical and political, towards a critical and unified understanding of reality. In the course of the historical process a new intellectual and moral order could evolve, an 'autonomous and superior culture' with 'more refined and decisive ideological weapons'. Gramsci's theory of hegemony attempts to raise some questions Marx had left unasked. What are the forms that ideological control takes? What is the relationship, and the difference, between ideological and political domination? Can we account for the multiplicity of ideologies, and for their rise and fall? In what sense, if any, do people *choose* to believe in an ideology? With these questions on the agenda, a range of possible answers would be provided during the remainder of the 20th century.

Gramsci's theory of hegemony notwithstanding, his role is retrospectively more important for another aspect of analysing ideology. As against the abstract and rarefied nature of the Marxist conception of ideology, exposed as a way of concealing and inhibiting correct social practices, Gramsci sought to explore the working of ideology as a practice in the world. We might refer to ideology as a thought-practice. This simply means a recurring pattern of (political) thinking, one for which there is evidence in the concrete world. The evidence for our thinking lies in our actions and utterances. Our thought-practices intermesh with, and inform, material and observable practices and acts. Sometimes it makes more sense to trace a movement from theory to practice; at other times the theory can be extracted from the practice itself. We are always looking at a two-way street.

For example, a belief in free choice is a recurring pattern among liberals, applied to innumerable situations such as voting, shopping, or choosing a partner. In the case of voting it can be held as a conscious general ideological principle. Voting is a deliberate

4. Antonio Gramsci.

exercise of political choice at the heart of liberal ideologies, linked to the core notion of consent. Shopping is participation in economic free-market transactions, though shoppers are rarely aware that their practice embodies the principle of free trade. Selecting a partner for emotional and sexual relationships is a conscious ideological thought-practice only when put in the context of arranged marriages. Otherwise it is an ideologically unconscious practice that has to be decoded by analysts as an embodiment of the voluntary principle. We do not choose partners just because we wish to demonstrate our adherence to the principle of free choice, but it is a largely invisible instance of such choice. The upshot of all this is to see ideologies as located in concrete activities, not as floating in a stratosphere high above them. The dichotomy between doing and thinking is challenged, for thinking is an activity that displays its own regularities. Political thinking is evident in reflection on how to organize collective behaviour, but it may also be retrieved through unpacking empirically observable acts.

Marx and Engels had dismissed German philosophy as a metaphysical form of ideology, practised by a few professionals. Gramsci sought to bring philosophy down to earth by suggesting that most people were philosophers in so far as they engaged in practical activity, activity constrained by views of the world they inhabited. At a stroke, Gramsci demystified philosophy and reintegrated it into the normal thought-processes of individuals. He did this, however, while retaining a threefold structure of political thought. There were individual philosophies generated by philosophers; broader philosophical cultures articulated by leading groups; and popular 'religions' or faiths. The second type was an embodiment of hegemony, and displayed the features of coherence and critique that hegemonic groups eventually imposed on the thinking under their control. The third type existed in embryonic form among the masses, for whom general conceptions of the world emerged in sudden and fragmented flashes. Importantly for Gramsci, each of these three levels could be combined in varying proportions to produce a different ideological cocktail. The distinction between the philosophical and the ideological began to evaporate the moment political thought was situated in the concrete world and directed at it.

What do we know about ideology, with Gramsci's help, that we might not have known before? As with Mannheim, Gramsci elevated ideology to the status of a distinct phenomenon worthy of, and open to, study. It inhabited a broad political arena that included moral and cultural norms and understandings, disseminated through the mass media and voluntary associations. And quite crucially it was to be found at various levels of articulation. True, ideology tended to a unity – central to the consensus and solidarity it forged – because the leading intellectuals of a given period subjugated other intellectuals through the attraction of their ideas, and directed the masses. These intellectuals, unlike Mannheim's, did not dispense with ideology; their mission was to modify it in line with the needs of the time. Part of such a modification would reflect the common sense of the masses, 'implicitly manifest in art, in law, in economic activity and in all manifestations of individual and collective life'.

Ultimately, Gramsci leaves us somewhat unsure of the nature of ideology, but he equips us with tools that enable us to proceed further. He confusingly vacillated between the Marxist view of ideology as dogma and a valiant attempt to release ideology from its negative connotations. He regarded ideology as achieving unity within a 'social bloc' – a cohesive social group – and held out hope for a total and homogeneous ideology that would attain social truth, while urging us to take current instances of ideology seriously. Even more than with Mannheim, a unified expression of the social world would emerge out of ideological pluralism. But Gramsci had a good grasp of the concrete and diverse forms in which ideology presented itself, in particular of its qualitatively variable voices. If Marx and Engels wished us to disregard the airy-fairy thoughts of intellectuals, and if Mannheim wished to reconstitute the intelligentsia as a source of unbiased theorizing about society,

Gramsci recognized the role of popular thinking in dialogue with the intelligentsia, producing the kind of complex ideological positions that characterize the modern world.

The reality of ideology: Louis Althusser

The place of Louis Althusser, the French Marxist philosopher and academic (1918–90), in the development of theories of ideology is somewhat less significant than Mannheim's or Gramsci's, although Althusser is regarded as a major redefiner of ideology within the Marxist tradition. Althusser followed Marx in assigning the ruling ideology the role of ensuring the submission of the workers to the ruling class. That was achieved by disseminating the rules of morality and respect required to uphold the established order. Official 'apparatuses' such as the state, the church, and the military practised control over the 'know-how' that was necessary to secure repression and ensure the viability of the existing economic system. But Althusser departed from Marx in acknowledging that ideology was a 'new reality' rather than the obscuring of reality. He likened the ideological superstructure to the top storey of a three-storied house. It was superimposed on the economic and productive base – the ground floor – and on the middle floor, the political and legal institutions. These were also part of the superstructure, but one that intervened directly in the base. Although the upper floors were held up by the base, they exercised 'relative autonomy'.

Effectively, the repressive state apparatus was the dominating political force, but ideology developed a life of its own as the symbolic controller. The ideological state apparatuses were located in religious, legal, and cultural structures, in the mass media and the family, and especially in the educational system. One input of Althusser into changing understandings of ideology was to recognize the variety of its institutional forms – the multiplicity of ideological apparatuses as against the singularity of the illusion that Marx and Engels had decried. A second input was to acknowledge the widespread dispersal of ideology beyond the public sphere to

5. Louis Althusser.

the private (Althusser did not distinguish between the private area of the family and the broader civil sphere). Political views of the world were present in all walks of life. But as with so many other Marxists, this was a qualified plurality: ideology was plural only in its location in diverse social spheres. It was not plural in its functions, retaining only the Marxist function of exercising unified hegemonic power so as to maintain existing capitalist relations of exploitation. Althusser refused to be drawn into formulating a theory of particular ideologies, nor was he interested in aspects of ideology that were unrelated to oppressive power.

A third input was the insistence that ideology has fundamental features irrespective of the historical forms specific ideologies adopt. It is one with which contemporary scholars of ideology have much sympathy. Unlike Marx and Engels, Althusser declared that 'ideology is eternal'. By that he meant that individuals inevitably think about the real conditions of their existence in a particular manner: they produce an imaginary account of how they relate to the real world. Ideology was a representation, an image, of those relations. For example, to describe certain nations as freedom-loving may allude to existing practices in their countries that suggest that individuals do not want to be ruled over arbitrarily: elections, a free press, a judiciary that can regulate the executive. But at the same time, the phrase 'freedom-loving' is rich with ideological import. It is an imaginary representation of a nation as a crusader for such freedoms, even when that crusade involves war and intervention in other people's freedoms, and serves to promote the economic interests of that nation. Ideology permits societies to imagine that such actions really do further the cause of freedom. It provides a view of their real world that explains it and reconciles them to it. Ideology does that by obscuring from a society the illusory and (favoured Marxist term) distorted nature of that representation. Ideology is inevitable because our imaginations cannot avoid such distortions.

Althusser's fourth input was to suggest that ideology exists in a material form in social practices, or in the institutions he called social apparatuses. From a Marxist perspective, this was an intriguing statement, as it implied that ideologies were, contra the early Marx, located in the material world – the world that mattered! The ideological understandings that propelled individual activities, even if those understandings 'distorted' imaginary representations,

6. Diego Rivera's 'Man controller of the universe' symbolizes both the desire of human beings to dominate others, and the difficulty any hegemonic ideology would experience in managing social diversity.

actually existed. Ideologies were not just the illusory contortions of a camera obscura reflecting the distorted consciousness of individual subjects, but an aspect of reality. Ideas existed in actions – an observation Gramsci had made in a slightly different way. We had to respect the ideologically inspired provenance of individual actions, even if we knew they did not reflect proper human relations. After all, those were precisely the actions that people performed in the real world. Many of those actions were rituals on which the human imagination conferred social significance: football matches, harvest celebrations, political party conferences, or religious worship. For Althusser, somewhat controversially, even thinking was a material practice, in that it actually took place. He referred to external verbal discourses (speeches and texts, one presumes) but also to 'internal' verbal discourse (consciousness). That insight further opened up the possibility for analysts of ideology to claim that political thinking was a central feature of the empirical regularities of political life.

Finally, Althusser's fifth input was that concrete individual subjects were made to serve as carriers of ideology, thus severing the inevitability of its link with class as proclaimed by earlier Marxists. For that reason, the very notion of ideology itself depended on the ideological concept of the subject – individuals constituted by ideology as bearers of consciousness, will, and agency. In other words, 'ideology' and 'subject' were mutually defining. If I acted as an individual who desired, say, to marry and have a fulfilling and lucrative career, I was putting my private life-purposes at the centre of my world, and others were recognizing my right to do that. But at the same time I was the product of an ideology that caused me to think of myself as a free agent whose fulfilment would be in a long-term, formalized relationship with another individual designated as 'spouse', and in a profitable activity that would secure the means of purchasing the labour and products of others. I lived 'naturally' in such an ideology and believed that I was acting spontaneously and autonomously.

The phrase Althusser used to explain the relationship between subject and ideology is 'interpellating' or naming. Althusser repudiated the abstractness of ideology, as well as its status solely as a group product. He enabled future students of ideology to appreciate that ideology is both something that happens *in* us and *to* us. Inasmuch as it is in us, we are not fully conscious of its effects. But if we are sufficiently astute, we can acknowledge that we identify each other through ideology, as individuals possessing certain features rather than others. That is a process of mutual recognition that brings order in its wake, such as 'you are a greengrocer, I am a customer', and, underpinning that, an awareness that is not always evident: 'we are both subject to the rules of the market'. The ambiguity of the term 'subject', Althusser argued, catches the essence of ideology beautifully. It refers to the free initiative of the individual, but also to the domination of the individual by a higher authority. For instance, being entrepreneurial, cowardly, caring – all these are particular features that our ideological imaginations deem important for one reason or another. These are all categories we apply in order to make sense of human actions. They all define the characteristics of individual subjects, thus placing them within a recognizable social network. They are all linked to practices of which we approve or disapprove, but which occur in the real world. Ultimately – and crucially – all these are *permanent* aspects of social life.

Chapter 3
Ideology at the crossroads of theory

Exploring the reasons why ideology came to stay as a category of political and philosophical analysis tells only part of the story. Concrete historical developments sustained the interest in ideologies more than the thoughts, however illuminating, of a few theorists. Both Gramsci and Althusser might have appreciated that. The advent of mass politics in Europe saw the consolidation of traditions of political thought such as liberalism, conservatism, and socialism. These complex movements and frameworks for political debate began to develop a life of their own, through the tenacity of their survival and through the front-line role they began to play in political decision-making. Ideologies, from this perspective, were political traditions that impelled individuals and groups to political action, and some of them exercised a huge impact on the formation of public policies and even on the fortunes of the states in which they prevailed. That process was aided by the close relationship established by political parties with these traditions of thinking. The people who promoted those traditions were not always keen to call them by the name 'ideologies' but ideologies they certainly were, though only in selective senses of the foregoing discussion. Indeed, while their promoters were bereft of a *theory* of ideology, the ideologies themselves amassed colossal influence through the development of programmatic politics: the introduction of party manifestos in the late 19th century, and the emergence of practical political thinkers who reinterpreted politics not only as a battle among power holders and notables, not even solely as a clash of selfish and avaricious interests, but as a struggle over the minds of men and women.

Towards a definition: the functions of ideology

A sensible way of comprehending the ideological belief systems that were organized around political traditions is to adopt a functional approach, that is, to identify the role they play in political life. Accordingly, here is a provisional definition that will be added to below:

> **A political ideology is a set of ideas, beliefs, opinions, and values that**
>
> (1) **exhibit a recurring pattern**
> (2) **are held by significant groups**
> (3) **compete over providing and controlling plans for public policy**
> (4) **do so with the aim of justifying, contesting or changing the social and political arrangements and processes of a political community.**

Let us unpack this definition.

The requirement of a recurring pattern is politically important. It signals that we are talking about traditions with staying power, not referring merely to idiosyncratic 'flash-in-the-pan' schemes, and that political institutions and practices can be sustained that intersect with the ideology in question. Liberalism, for instance, developed around the insistence of rising social classes on freeing themselves of despotic domination by ruling groups, and through the flowering of cultural views, associated with the Enlightenment, that put creative individuals at the centre of the world. Liberal parties emerged quite some time after those initial triggers, but persevered in demands to extend liberty and choice to marginalized groups and to break down barriers that impeded human opportunities. That proved to be a long-term project that even now is far from complete. And while an ideology and a party sharing the same name are never identical, they are mutually supportive. The pattern itself, as we shall note at the end of the chapter, will be flexible rather than rigid.

The requirement that an ideology be held by significant groups alludes to its origins and to its contestability in a plural and contentious political world. Ideologies may, as Althusser claimed, be carried by conscious individuals, but they are, as Mannheim realized, social products. The significance of ideological producers is not easy to ascertain. We saw in the previous chapter that intellectuals are often identified as the authors of an ideology, but neither Gramsci nor Mannheim raised the possibility of there being different types of intellectual groups. In France, unlike the UK or the USA, intellectuals have maintained a strong presence in the political world. However, other significant groups have increasingly come into play. Significance may refer to the ability to control the media or to serve as political spin doctors, rather than to the relation of the group to the means of production. Or it may refer to the non-verbal communicative skills that now match verbal skills – advertising, logos, documentaries, symbols of colour and shape (a yellow ribbon, a red flag). In addition, interest and pressure groups may subscribe to a segment of an ideology – say the rights of pensioners. That segment will be part of a larger ideological family in which rights are promoted and redistribution to the disadvantaged is advocated. More amorphous and widespread support of the kind Gramsci discussed may be embedded in populist sentiment and opinion; for example, a refusal, on the basis of religious beliefs, to endorse the equal treatment of women. We shall return to these themes below.

Significance is ultimately a question of the political clout and the social import assigned to the relevant ideological producer. But it reminds us that in the main politics is about a range of different values and about the contests that occur not among individuals but among larger human groupings. Ideologies reflect the rise and fall of groups along with changing fortunes and criteria of significance: being born into the aristocracy no longer guarantees one's ideas a podium, as in the days of old. This may prompt a search for new support. Conservative parties, for example, adjusted to the loss of old social bases by appealing successfully to groups united on religious interests (European Christian Democracy, sections of the US Republican Party), on popular attitudes (anti-immigration, patriotism), and on the preservation of economic ascendancy (big business).

The requirement of competing over public policy reminds us that we are dealing with *political* ideologies. Ideologies are aimed at the public arena, and they usually are in contention over drawing up macro-programmes (as in party-political manifestos) for social and economic policy and for effective administration. Not every group plan is an ideology, but it may be interpreted as a part of larger ideological designs. The governors of a school may draw up plans for changing the pattern of intake of pupils, but that is not an ideology in the 'grand traditions' sense. It could, however, align itself with a particular ideology's view of social integration.

Finally, ideologies are major exercises in swaying key political decision-makers as well as public opinion. Political actors are recruited through ideologies to important causes with immense practical consequences. In countries enjoying open politics, ideologies seek to justify their bids for support through activities ranging from persuasion to propaganda. Socialist parties throughout the 20th century have enlisted such support by producing pamphlets for working-class people (the famous Fabian Tracts, for instance), by publishing their own newspapers, and by providing social services to their members when those services were unavailable or too expensive to purchase on the open market. Socialist parties have generally aimed to contest and change existing policies, but other ideologies are bent on preserving them against sudden and what they might call 'unnatural' change.

The end of ideology?

One problem for the analyst of ideologies is that many holders of ideology, especially but not solely conservatives, have denied that they are ideological. Instead they have seen themselves as pragmatic, reserving the appellation 'ideology' only for the ideas of those political movements that issue plans for radical and total change. This undoubtedly reflects the problem that open contestation, and consequently the need for justification, have been largely absent in the totalitarian regimes discussed in Chapter 6 – typically but not exclusively Nazi Germany and Stalinist Russia. Their tauter and more lethal ideologies were imposed through force and terror with little appeal to the critical rational faculties of their citizens and subjects. The pernicious and virulent impact of these two regimes conferred undue salience on the variants of fascism and communism they advanced, and encouraged the general propensity to identify their features with those of ideologies in general. Hence learned treatises on 'The age of ideologies' misleadingly implied that only those closed and superimposed systems of ideas and practices qualified as ideologies, while conservatism, liberalism, and socialism were 'non-ideological'.

The climax of this popular rejection of ideology was spearheaded by the attempt of several reputable scholars to declare the end of ideology in the 1950s and 1960s. This stark rejection of ideology was the product both of the historical interpretation adopted by these scholars – and their mimics in the mass media – and of the espousal of an even more restrictive theory of ideology than the one that had emerged from Marxism. They believed that the defeat of the totalitarian regimes signalled the demise of brutal strife for world ideological domination. Rather, both Russians and Americans sought a consumer-oriented society and aspired to similar creature comforts. The result would be a convergence between previously hostile world-views, dictated by the necessities of good living. This view appeared plausible at the time. After the

7. This is the Road.

ideological 'over-heating' of the 1930s and 1940s, the 1950s seemed particularly sterile. Western societies were emerging from a devastating war, while the granting of independence for European colonies was only beginning. Economic stability by means of a mixed economy was a major political goal. On the positive side, great strides had been made in establishing welfare states in Europe but, in ideological terms, this created the impression of consensus politics and the termination of divergence over principles.

The end-of-ideology theorists were taken in by a series of delusions. The first was a logical error. If conservatives, liberals, and socialists all agreed on implementing the principles of the welfare state – namely, a state supported redistribution of social goods and the underpinning of human flourishing as a central political aim – this did not imply the end of ideology but the confluence of many ideological positions on a single point. There could still be a (more or less) common ideology of the welfare state. The second was a faulty historical prediction. The 1960s were about to witness an explosion of new ideological variants, particularly in the Third World. African socialisms, Indonesian guided democracy, pan-Arabism, all these now entered the political arena, demonstrating the ingenuity of the human mind in devising new forms of socio-political thought.

The third was an analytical mistake. Ideologies do not only diverge over grand principles but also over peripheral and detailed practices. Even were we to assume complete agreement on the principles of the welfare state, ideological dissent could simply be deflected to what may seem to be technical questions: (*a*) how do we raise the money for welfare services? (*b*) which groups should receive priority in obtaining state help, given that budgets are always limited? These questions, however, clearly elicit a plethora of different ideological solutions. Direct taxation or indirect taxation involve divergent principles. The former may be graduated, making the rich pay proportionately more. The latter could impose a similar tax on rich and poor, thus becoming a regressive rather than a progressive tax. Who should get help first is a question of sorting out priorities: do the young have precedence over the very old? The unemployed over the sick? The physically disabled over the mentally disabled? Single mothers over asylum seekers? These all are major ideological distinctions that reflect very different understandings of the values involved in policy-making.

In response to question (*a*), assuming that welfare states promote some form of equality, equality emerges as the proportional ability to bear a financial burden; and the advocacy of redistribution from rich to poor, given an original unfair distribution. Here is one set of issues that centrally concerns all ideologies: which pattern to adopt in distributing scarce social goods? In response to question (*b*) we have a competition among needy groups, all with legitimate claims for assistance in coping with life circumstances over which they have very limited control. This set of issues, too, centrally concerns all ideologies: how to prioritize competing claims from deserving or vulnerable groups while maintaining the vital political support without which an ideology may flounder.

The 'end of ideology' was in several ways also a retrogressive *theoretical* stance. It reverted to endowing ideology with an aura of apocalyptic thinking, the unfolding of an historical truth with scientific pretensions, a method of social engineering, and the passion of a secular religion. It picked up the thread that saw ideology as the creation of intellectuals as 'priests', derogatorily depicted as distanced from society and pursuing 'pure' thought. For one of its main detractors, Daniel Bell, ideology was an 'irretrievably fallen word'; for another, Edward Shils, ideologies were always alienated from their societies and always demanded individual subservience to them. The Marxist conception had apparently brought Western theories of ideology to a dead end. That overlooked the subtle insights that Mannheim, Gramsci, and Althusser had in their different ways enabled the concept of ideology to acquire; indeed, it overlooked the subtleties that Marx himself had developed on the topic. Contra the 'end of ideology' advocates, the usefulness of the *notion* of ideology – let alone the actual systems of ideas signified by that notion – was still clearly evident. While some avenues appeared to close, others were opening up.

Mass attitudes and beliefs

The development of the social sciences in the United States brought in its wake a non-Marxist view of ideology, removed from the theoretical concerns that preoccupied European scholars. The empirical bent of political science focused on field research, on the attitudes and opinions of the new mass publics that were attracting the increasing attention of the discipline. That process was further fuelled by the extolling of democratic politics and the 'common man', in part as an antidote to the dictatorial and elitist voices of the 1930s. Ideologies were now tantamount to political belief systems, and the task of the researcher was to describe them and to place them in categories that could be 'scientifically' generalized and, more often than not, measured. Statistical methods came into their own in exploring the distribution of beliefs, their aggregation, and variation. One could combine individual opinions – dispersed across a given population – into groupings that shared common experiences.

In this milieu ideologies were taken as explicitly known to their bearers – or, in psychological language, cognitive. The technique was known as behaviourist, that is, focusing on concrete and observable forms of human conduct, not on broader social forces or unconsciously held worldviews. Ideologies were, moreover, assumed to contain not only factual information about a political system but moral beliefs about human beings and their relation to society. Those were thought to hold the key to human action or inaction. Notwithstanding, that methodology was far more indebted to the sociology of the day than to philosophy. Furthermore, these belief systems were acknowledged to be 'emotionally charged' rationalizations and justifications, in the words of one of the key writers on this approach to ideology, Robert E. Lane. In sum, ideologies were there to be discovered by the keen social scientist.

Notably lacking was any sense of grand political and ideational schemes – after all, the role of American political parties did not include the disseminating of the great ideological traditions, as did their European counterparts. Instead, ideologies were thought to be rather unstructured and lacking analytical depth. We all held them as part of our psychological and mental equipment. Their study could enable scholars (and politicians) to take the attitudinal pulse of their societies and to draw their own conclusions. Left–right continuums, mimicking the seating arrangements made famous during the French Revolution, could be employed to gauge opinion on war and peace, social services, or political reform. Two-by-two boxes could help distinguish between authoritarian and democratic personalities married to either rational or irrational conduct, or correlated with a predilection for state planning versus free markets. None of these modelling devices could express the complexity of ideological structure and the interweaving of such categories. That application of the social sciences simplified life, and prevalent perceptions of ideologies were tarred with that simplicity. The potential of ideology as a pivotal organizing concept of political thought looked unpromising.

Ideology as symbol

At that point succour came from outside the discipline of politics. The borrowing and exchange of explanatory paradigms among disciplines is one of the most fertile ways of developing new thinking in a given field, and they paved alternative paths forward for interpreting the nature of ideology, giving its conceptualization a much-needed boost. The anthropologist Clifford Geertz wrote a seminal article in 1964, in which he portrayed ideologies as an ordered system of complex cultural symbols. These symbols acted as representations of reality and provided the maps without which individuals and groups could not orientate themselves with respect to their society. If one political system had frequent recourse to marches and military parades, these served as cultural symbols of national vigour. An ideology could then prioritize power over, say, welfare. If another political system blamed foreigners or a particular ethnic group in its midst for economic and social malaise, they too served as cultural symbols of certain behavioural traits that the members of that society envied, desired, or dissociated from themselves. An ideology could then displace internal political criticism onto those 'anti-social' symbols.

Geertz's contribution to the theory of ideology was to grasp that ideologies were metaphors that carried social meaning. Put differently, they were multilayered symbols of reality that brought together complex ideas. Take an ideology that, for example, advocated the importance of the ballot box. That concrete symbol could be employed as a rhetorical device locating ultimate decision-making in the people (though democratic theory may suggest otherwise). It could also be an emotional representation of why loyalty to the system should be forthcoming, and serve as an institutional deflection of political responsibility away from the leadership. The ballot box could also paper over contradictions and ambiguities. It combined the notion of devolved and accountable power with a situation of individual choice in which the voter was socially isolated from group consultation and accountable to no one. These conflicting elements of democracy were obscured through the symbolism of the ballot box.

For Geertz, the symbol-systems we call ideologies constituted maps of social reality. Maps, after all, are themselves symbols, simplifying the terrain through which they are intended to guide us. Maps are selective; they protect us from over-information that may be quite useless. If I wish to drive from London to Birmingham, I do not need to know every bump in the road, and I wouldn't be able to handle, physically or mentally, such a detailed map. It certainly wouldn't fit in the car. Ideological maps, however, are special kinds of maps. They have flexible notions of proximity between the components of the ideology. They may, for example, bind the idea of legitimacy to the institution of hereditary monarchy, or align it with the directives of a sacred text, or attach it to the seal of popular consent. We may consequently conclude that ideologies are symbolic devices that order social space. They tell us what to look out for but, as we noted in Chapter 1, there may be competing ideological maps for the same social reality, maps that trace different routes among the social principles and practices they detect. Thus, the encouraging of liberty may lead to individual development and be valued for that reason, but it may also lead to lifestyle choices that fly against conventional morality, and hence be condemned. The one may be a liberal path that trusts individuals to make rational use of their liberty; the other a conservative path that insists on social constraints and objects to individual experimentation.

In addition, ideologies also order social and historical time. Historical time is far from being a record of everything that 'happened'. It is a selective and patterned listing of events (some of which may even be mythical, such as the founding of Rome by Remus and Romulus) that are woven together to form an ideological narrative. English history has singled out landmarks such as the Magna Carta of 1215, the Glorious Revolution of 1688, and the several enfranchisement Acts between 1832 and 1918 as formative political experiences. That story – symbolizing England and later the UK as a nation with a strong heritage of liberty – is one of which UK citizens are expected to be proud, but it is only one of many stories we could tell about the history of this nation, not all of which would be flattering. A history of the role of women in the UK would produce a very different tale. In this capacity, ideologies are collections of symbolic signposts through which a collective national identity is forged.

Games families play

The philosopher Ludwig Wittgenstein also contributed importantly to the study of ideology, though his contribution was indirect and unintended. Wittgenstein argued that language was akin to a game, and a central characteristic of a game is that it has rules. Using a language meant learning its rules. Rules both permit and constrain; they may be general or highly specific. From this others deduced that ideologies, too, are a form of language game, whose meaning and communicative importance can only be determined by noting their grammar (the fundamental structures and patterns of relationship among their components), their conventional employment in a social context, and the degree of acceptability of the rules by which they play. I would only subscribe to Nazi doctrines if the rules of Nazism made sense to me. They would do so if I accepted that the word 'Aryan' was a desirable, and the word 'Jew' an undesirable, term for the features of a group. Moreover, the rules of that language game pitted Aryan against Jew as opposites. By further classifying Jews as 'subhuman', their elimination could not, by definition, be a crime against *humanity*.

A second significant argument of Wittgenstein's was that sets of features may be broadly similar without being identical in all respects. To explain that he used the phrase 'family resemblances'. It indicated that there were overlapping characteristics of a special kind among members of the same set. Say that the family resemblances included a wide forehead, thin lips, brown eyes, and fair hair. Family members would not necessarily have *all* these features, but in a large family any member would share something in common with some other members (if I had fair hair, another would too). However, there could still be two members who shared nothing in common (the one having a wide forehead, thin lips, blue eyes and ginger hair, the other having a narrow forehead, thick lips, brown eyes, and fair hair). This idea allowed analysts of ideology to develop a greater subtlety in investigating an ideological tradition. They could maintain that liberalism, for example, contained a number of internal variants that shared a range of overlapping as well as distinct properties. Far from being monolithic, the standard structure of an ideology was a jigsaw of components that furnished it with considerable flexibility. Different liberalisms shared several features while simultaneously playing host to separate elements. All liberalisms could promote individuality but some could be divided over the relative merits of private versus public ownership.

Wittgenstein also employed the analogy of a thread to illustrate that tradition changed over time in such a way that its continuity was more illusory than real. Just as a thread isn't an unbroken strand, but a series of overlapping fibres, so a tradition may have short-term continuities that vary so slowly and delicately that – unless we scrutinize their history – we fail to notice them.

Together, the two ideas allowed analysts to conceive of specific ideologies as relatively fluid arrangements that bunched together under a common name. Hence most changes in the detailed components of an ideology did not necessitate its renaming. Quite the opposite: such changes were normal and to be expected in any ideological family. No less importantly, the discovery of the internal fluidity of ideologies allowed them to be recast as engines of change and renewal, not just as unbending instruments of dominance. That was reinforced by some of the developments to which we now turn.

Chapter 4
The struggle over political language

Language and meaning

Developments in linguistics provided another external source of inspiration for students of ideology. The emphasis on grammar and on semantics (the study of meaning) opened new doors through which students of ideology began to rush in increasing numbers. Grammar was presented as the structural rules that linked words together in a particular sequence. Words, as we know, are not pieced together randomly (as in 'political all the free government should prisoners') but only 'made sense' in particular arrangements ('the government should free all political prisoners').

Similarly ideologies, which were expressed primarily through language, were seen as displaying their own grammatical peculiarities. Moreover, words – and combinations of words – carried specific meaning: their sounds and letters (the signs) indicated something else that was being represented, or signified. The word 'authority' might signify a series of acts of deference to a person or institution. But the meanings of words were also interdependent; they were located in a network of relationships with other words and were only intelligible in that context. The word 'free' meant something quite different in the sentence 'The government should free all political prisoners' and in the sentence 'Pop over and see me if you have some free time'. Not only did the rules of grammar establish that in the first case 'free' was a verb and in the second an adjective but, more importantly for our purposes, the relationships between the words in the two sentences established that what was being discussed was (*a*) an act of liberation, and (*b*) the absence of other commitments.

Students of ideology, who discovered rather late in the day that it was profitable to treat ideologies as linguistic and semantic products, turned their new knowledge to good use. The internal complexity of ideologies was perceived more clearly; especially the possibility that ideologies could carry a multiplicity of meanings through a minor tweaking of the words and phrases they utilized. Moreover, liaising with psychological insights, the impact of the unconscious was beginning to be felt. Grammar, after all, existed at an unconscious level for native users of a language. Likewise, ideological assumptions – concerning the meanings of the words and ideas to which we have recourse – could be held unknowingly. This was a major departure in the investigation of political thought. Political philosophers, particularly of the Anglo-American variety, have insisted on the reflective and purposive nature of political theory. Empirical students of ideology, as observed above, assumed it to be a cognitive activity, known to the bearers of an ideology. Unintentional messages had not seemed to be of scholarly significance because they were not subject to the rational control of the users of political language.

The surplus of meaning

The unconscious became an important object of ideological exploration, aided by several developments in post-war continental theorizing. One instance was the impact of the French philosopher Paul Ricoeur, whose extensive studies of ideology emphasized its positive as well as its negative sides. Ricoeur singled out one unconscious aspect of ideology that he termed a 'surplus of meaning'. By that he meant that ideologies (as indeed many forms of human expression) conveyed more information than their authors were aware of, or had intended. For example, when Machiavelli famously likened fortune to a woman who, in order to be submissive, had to be beaten and coerced, he intended that as a warning to princes to control the vicissitudes of fortune if they wanted to succeed. In so doing he employed a metaphor that would not have been unfamiliar to his readers. However, we now interpret that passage as reflecting an extremely unpleasant attitude to women, though this meaning is surplus to the points Machiavelli wished to make.

One lesson to be learnt from that is that ideologies are not only produced but consumed, and that their consumption is not identical from instance to instance. Ideologies are interpreted and understood by the populations to whom they are directed in many different ways. We know that the readings of the American Constitution with reference to the equal protection of the laws – in the abstract, a bedrock of the liberal notion of the rule of law – have varied considerably over time. One reading legitimated the principle of 'separate but equal' that justified the segregation of black and white populations. A later reading demanded the integration of those populations. These unlimited readings can occur contemporaneously: the ideology of welfarism was understood by conservatives to support industrial peace and productivity, and by socialists to hold out the promise of social solidarity and the fairer redistribution of scarce goods. The study of such variable readings is known as reception theory.

At the same time, the producers of ideology are not alone in being unaware of the surplus of meaning they produce. Crucially, its consumers may absorb frameworks of understanding, whose messages and consequences are undetectable to *them*. One such process is the socialization of the very young. When the awareness of an infant is crystallizing, it perceives the world as authoritarian, unequal, and hierarchical. That is not because adults behave improperly to babies and toddlers, but results from the physical size of adults, and from the necessary imposition of order and decision-making on those not yet capable of running their own lives. Views of the political we normally associate with totalitarianism and with many types of conservatism – the naturalness of accepting orders and direction from an external source, the inevitability of leadership, the relative insignificance of the individual in relation to society – constitute the initial *political* impressions in all societies. Most societies prefer to leave their members in that state of political infantilism by refusing to re-educate them in alternative modes of conduct. A particular ideological view of the world becomes ingrained and hence invisible. The divine right of kings, the supremacy of a sacred religious text, the benevolent wisdom of the rulers, the futility of challenging fate, beliefs which themselves may be consciously held, contain such surpluses of meaning. A few societies attempt to resocialize their young at a later stage and encourage them – within carefully confined limits – to challenge authority, to promote social equality, and to be wary of some hierarchies; in short, to think critically for themselves. But even in such societies, the outcome is only the establishment of a few pockets of people disposed to realize those liberal precepts. For most people, the liberal preference for continuously revising and re-evaluating one's plans of life may be too much of a burden. Even for liberals, many of their sacred cows, such as the right to choose your own profession, are also taken for granted, rather than appreciated as an unusual gift of autonomy.

Making sense of ideological texts

The hermeneutic school – the study of interpretation – brought its own benefits to studying ideology. One guideline of hermeneutics is that the meaning of texts can only be decoded if we are able to tap into the contexts in which the text was written and in which it would make sense. An ideology, too, is a text – an argument, a statement, a narrative, an appeal – whether written or oral (though, as we shall see, ideologies also possess non-textual dimensions). Thus, liberalism as expressed in the 1940s and 1950s by Isaiah Berlin, Karl Popper, or Jacob Talmon, emphasized negative liberty.

It preferred the absence of deliberate intervention in a person's actions to a conception of liberty that allowed the state to intervene and regulate the conduct of individuals in order to release, or free, their potential. For this ideological reading of liberty to be properly understood it has to be set against the background of the oppressive totalitarian regimes to which these thinkers reacted. This aspect of hermeneutics dovetails with Mannheim's emphasis on the social conditioning of ideology.

Another guideline of hermeneutics refers to the texts themselves. Texts open up manifold possibilities for their comprehension – they do not sanction one authoritative reading. The main reason for that is that the meanings of words, sentences, and by extension, ideologies, cannot be pinned down unequivocally. The multiple meanings they carry, their polysemy, forever render them indeterminate. A radical version of this standpoint was captured in the phrase 'the authorless text'. Once a text was produced, the argument went, it embarked on a life of its own, subject to the understandings of its diverse future readers, rather than the control of its author. This idea threw a lifeline of great importance to analysts of ideology. The realization that ideologies – as texts – contained infinitely variable forms reinforced the argument that the term 'ideology' in the singular could no longer be employed to substitute for the multiple ideologies it concealed. However, polysemy could be taken too far. Its theoretical boundlessness was none other than an abstract logical property of texts. It suggested that we could never ascertain all the meanings that an ideology could carry, which may be true, but it offered no criteria on how to select the more significant from the less significant variants. That made it impossible to get a handle on the real world of ideologies. If there are infinite interpretations, all of which are valid simply because they make sense under certain conditions, how can we ever understand, let alone appraise, an ideology?

The response to that problem came from some theorists of ideology who contended that cultural and historical constraints narrow down that indeterminacy considerably. Although we may always offer a new reading to an ideology, we need to take into account that the formulators of ideologies have ploughed distinct furrows and have made their specific marks on the field. As we have seen, the accumulative history of extant ideologies with their own staying power – conservatism, liberalism, or socialism – encouraged the major ideological movements to focus on a certain range of meanings and arguments, encompassed in a tradition, rather than to appear in inchoate and discontinuous forms. Questions such as individual liberty, the limits on state activity, or what to do with the poor, reappeared in many ideologies and obliged them to organize around those issues instead of others. From the standpoint of a given ideology this narrowing went even further, as the typical arguments of each ideology are presented in language that attempts to be as determinate as possible.

The way was now open to regard ideologies as devices specifically capable of coping with the indeterminacy of the political messages that circulated in a society. They handled that indeterminacy by selecting, privileging, and prioritizing certain social meanings among all those available, using various mixtures of persuasiveness, cajoling, and verbal force. Whereas, for example, the concept of change logically carried a host of meanings, conservatives attached the qualifiers 'gradual', 'safe', or 'natural' to the notion of change they wished to legitimate, while barring the qualifiers 'radical', 'revolutionary', and occasionally even 'planned'. There were thus three steps in analysing ideologies. The logic of the *category* 'ideology' was to acknowledge its limitless forms, reflecting the impossibility of pinning down meaning. Historical and cultural contexts, however, constricted the *range* of meanings from which to choose. Subsequently came the further observation: within that constricted range, any *particular* ideology tried to behave as if meaning could be made determinate. The question now became, how did ideologies actually go about whatever it was they were doing?

Ideological morphology: decontesting the contestable

Ideologies were accordingly presented from a perspective that illuminated them afresh. Just as sentences contain words in a particular pattern of interdependence, a pattern that enables us to make sense of the words, so it is with ideologies. Ideologies contain special words such as liberty, authority, equality, rights, and democracy. These words signify political concepts. Indeed, political concepts such as these are the basic units of political thought in general, of political philosophy as well as ideology. And ideologies assemble those political concepts in particular patterns. Liberalism, for example, always placed fundamental concepts such as liberty, individuality, rationality, and progress at its core. Other political concepts such as legitimacy and authority were made to be dependent on accommodating the core ones. The only *legitimate* government would then be one that respected individual *liberty*. Socialism had conceptual configurations surrounding the core concepts of group solidarity, equality, and labour. These fundamental concepts controlled the admission of other concepts into the socialist ideological family. Power had to further the ends of social equality; the individual was defined as a cooperative member of a group.

This perspective on ideology is the morphological approach. It is morphological because it sees the internal structure of ideologies as a vital aspect of their analysis. On this view, we can add another dimension to the previous characterizations of ideology in Chapter 3:

> **Ideologies are complex combinations and clusters of political concepts in sustainable patterns.**

The meanings conveyed by an ideology will therefore reflect the relationships among the concepts it hosts. Justice will possess a very different meaning if an ideology places it in close proximity to equality rather than to property. In the first case justice will always conjure up some form of equality – equality before the law, economic equality, gender equality, and the like – while in the second it will always have to nod in the direction of property – protecting it through laws of inheritance or through banning invasive taxation. This may further refine the understandings of ideology at our disposal. The meanings an ideology conveys reflect not only the historical traditions of political discourse, nor only the cultural pluralism of the different contexts in which the ideology is shaped, but can be accessed through the particular patterns in which its constituent political concepts are ordered. We now need to extend our characterization of an ideology as follows.

> **An ideology is a wide-ranging structural arrangement that attributes meaning to a range of mutually defining political concepts.**

An ideology is like a set of modular units of furniture that can be assembled in many ways (though some ways of arranging them would be too ridiculous to contemplate). Through diverse arrangements of the furniture we can create very different rooms, even by using the same units. That is why identical political concepts can serve as the building blocks of an entire series of disparate ideologies, for the same unit (concept) may have a different role (meaning) in two separate rooms (or ideologies). In one room a table will be used for dining; and in another for writing. In one ideology rights may be used to protect human dignity from assault; in another to protect private property and wealth from having to contribute to the common good.

Another way of understanding this approach is to relate ideologies to a well-known problem in the study of political thought: the 'essential contestability' of concepts. It consists of two propositions. The first is that we can never agree on an absolutely correct evaluation of a political concept. It makes no more sense to state definitively that 'liberty is better than equality' than to maintain that 'red is better than blue'. The first example may be an ethical judgement and the second an aesthetic one, but in neither case is there a universally accepted hierarchy of values that would permit a final assessment of the goods in question, nor can there ever be such a hierarchy, as we have no means of validating these preferences objectively.

The second proposition is that a political concept always contains more potential components than can be included in any actual definition or deployment of that concept. Consequently, one political *concept* will contain manifold *conceptions*. Take the concept of equality. If we think about it logically, in the abstract, it may refer to mathematical identity, to similarity, or to the moral equivalence of members of a specified group. It can be cashed out as equality of opportunity, or as equality of merit, or as equality of need. But no usage of the term 'equality' can convey all these meanings simultaneously, because some of them are mutually exclusive. A person cannot be identical to another and similar to her at the same time; nor can the notion of equality enjoin one to distribute a scarce good – say food – according to need (invoking criteria of hunger, fragility, or health requirements = all needs should be treated equally) while concurrently distributing it according to merit (invoking criteria of desert: 'I earned this food through hard work and you didn't' = all effort should have an equal claim). The essential contestability here lies in the fact that we can never agree on which of these understandings of equality should be included in the concept and which excluded from it. It is *essential* rather than *contingent* contestability because the polysemy of language will never permit it to be reduced to a single agreed meaning. There exists no laboratory of philosophical boffins aiming to crack this problem by the year 2020!

Ideologies are consequently the systems of thought through which specific meaning is conferred upon every political concept in their domain. That is achieved by legitimating one meaning of each concept and delegitimating the others. On their own, political concepts are too vague and too vacuous to carry intelligible meaning. If I get up and shout 'I demand freedom!' my cry remains incomprehensible. We immediately have to add detail that can only be supplied by answering further questions. Freedom from whom or what? How can we determine that I am free? What will I be doing or saying in exercising my freedom? *Do* I have to exercise anything when I am free? Consequently, adjacent concepts need to flesh out the concept of freedom. I may have to specify that I shall be free when no one interferes with me bodily, or when my rational desires and plans of life are not arbitrarily restricted but enabled through the cooperation of others. In the first case freedom is adjacent to a conception of the individual as occupying privileged private space, and to a conception of the state as limited in its interference in personal life. In the second case it is adjacent to a conception of the individual as a developing and purposive entity, and to the state as an enabling institution that reflects the mutual interdependence of individuals in a society.

An ideology specifies the meanings of the political concepts it contains by assembling them in a pattern that links them together with other specific concepts. This configuration teases out specific conceptions of each of the concepts involved. Its precision of meaning, while never conclusive, is gained by this specific and constricted interaction among the concepts it employs. An ideology attempts to end the inevitable contention over concepts by *decontesting* them, by removing their meanings from contest. 'This is what justice means', announces one ideology, 'and that is what democracy entails'. By trying to convince us that they are right and that they speak the truth, ideologies become devices for coping with the indeterminacy of meaning. That is their semantic role. Hence a minor modification to the previous characterization:

> **An ideology is a wide-ranging structural arrangement that attributes *decontested* meanings to a range of mutually defining political concepts.**

Ideologies also need to decontest the concepts they use because they are instruments for fashioning collective decisions. That is their political role. Without the introduction of specificity into a debate, such decisions cannot be taken. A decision is an expression of finality (real or manufactured) signalling the closure of discussion, and ideologies strive to provide the certainty that underpins such finality. In that way the producers of ideologies claim to champion the 'correct' meanings of the political concepts to which they refer. We need therefore to append another rider to our characterization of ideologies:

> Ideologies compete over the control of political language as well as competing over plans for public policy; indeed, their competition over plans for public policy is primarily conducted through their competition over the control of political language.

One lesson we may derive from the study of semantics is that whoever exercises such control is in a strong position to determine the political practices that members of a society will consider, or at least be capable of imagining. Once again, that struggle over control places ideologies at the heart of the political process.

Logical and cultural constraints

More needs to be said about the manner in which ideologies decontest the meanings of the political concepts at their disposal. Two types of constraint, logical and cultural, set the limits on the conscious or unconscious meanings that ideologies communicate. Logical constraints operate on all ideologies. It would be logically inconsistent for an ideology to defend individual choice and to deny people the vote, or to support greater social equality and to tax only low-income groups. Even ideologies conventionally deemed to be broadly irrational, such as fascism, possess a grim internal consistency once one passes through the looking-glass of their perverse worlds and proceeds to work from their fundamental assumptions. *If* Jews contaminate the Aryan race, and *if* such 'contamination' is detrimental to the good of the human race (two 'ifs' that do not stand serious rational scrutiny), *then* it makes sense to keep Jews apart from Aryans. As a matter of fact, all ideologies begin with non-negotiable assumptions from which logical conclusions can be drawn, but most of those assumptions – unlike fascist ones – are tolerable and can be given some rational or ethical justification. Thus, liberalism is not prepared to negotiate or to compromise over human rights allocated to individuals, or over the desirability of individual liberty. These can be justified through systems of morality that have also been seen to improve empirically people's quality of life.

None the less, logical inconsistencies do creep into ideologies. It is then that their attempt to control political language comes into its own. An ideology may contend that it wishes to promote major environmental reforms that will reduce the risk of global warming, while concurrently advocating a policy of investment in polluting industries. Ideologies are adept at reconciling such tensions mainly because the polysemic manner in which each of these two policies is formulated allows for enough interpretative leeway to find an area of logical consistency among them. The ideology may insert a policy of taxing polluters and utilizing those funds for environmental research, arguing that zero pollution is always impossible. Or it may introduce a time-scale, maintaining that other ideological principles – gradualism, respect for current property rights – intervene and require protection as well. Or it may produce empirical evidence to the effect that the pollution created by national industries contributes quite insignificantly to global warming. The opportunities are legion, and not all of them are cynical manipulations of information sent out to the public.

In effect, vagueness and elusiveness are frequently necessary to, and functional in, the political arena. Politics consists not only of decision-making, which demands decontestation, but also of the mobilization of support. The latter requires the construction of consensus, or at least the corralling of members of a society into overlapping positions in order to optimize backing for a political stance. In those situations, consumers of political language must be offered sentences that are sufficiently open in their meaning for different individuals and groups to read into them their own preferences and to gloss over distinctions. When a politician announces that he wishes to encourage the values of community, the moving of that concept to the centre of the ideological room will please many ideological consumers. It will please socialists, for whom the notion of community is associated with social solidarity and the importance of group activity. It will please conservatives, for whom the notion of community is associated with the collective wisdom of accumulative generations and the settled ways of existing concrete small communities. It will even please some environmentalists, for whom the interconnectedness of nature must be mirrored in the holistic interlocking of social life.

Hence ambiguity as well as certainty are two necessary features of any ideology. They extend its life expectancy, and are vital to the (imagined) harmony and stability normally sought through the political process. This may give a bad name to politics, but elusiveness is not simply dissimulation, trickery, or sloppy thinking – though it may be any of these – but the harnessing of political language in order to provide one of the most valuable scarce resources of politics: public political backing. In any case, the precision of language is never guaranteed, and even strong decontestation will be open to many interpretations. Some unanticipated, as well as anticipated, interpretations may of course reduce support rather than increasing it. The British Conservative Party's decision to promote 'family values' backfired when it was decontested, inter alia, as marital fidelity (which not all conservative politicians exhibited) rather than, say, as altruism and care for others.

Moving to cultural constraints, we may note that culture refers to the symbolic and material goods that societies produce. Those will include artefacts, science and technology, art, and social practices. It involves imaginative creativity and encompasses the systems of ideas and of thought that order our worlds and direct our conduct and activities. The cultural constraints on ideologies serve to anchor them firmly into the contexts of time and space, and to fine-tune the logical interpretations that their conceptual arrangements can carry. Take for instance the question of how to eradicate poverty in a particular country. Logically we have a very broad range of possibilities. One solution would be to exterminate the poor. Another would be to transport them to Ruritania – we might call that economic cleansing! A third would be to redefine the concept of poverty so as to exclude the entire living population, say by claiming that we are impoverished only at the point of death. A fourth would be to pre-empt the unequal distribution of resources in the first place, by designing a society in which members contribute to a common pool according to their abilities and extract from it according to their needs (given sufficient resources in the first place). A fifth would be to redistribute resources from the better- to the worse-off.

The first two options are not open to civilized societies: morality and decency, as well as practical considerations, render them culturally invalid. Logic, however, is quite blind to questions of good or evil. The third is an attempt to reconceptualize poverty, but it flies in the face of common-sense usages of the term – another cultural constraint that ideologies would ignore at their peril. Nor would it remove the fact that many people cannot make ends meet: we would simply need to coin a new term for what used to be called poverty. The fourth option envisages an organizational and ideological revolution. It might happen, but would require a major political upheaval. The fifth option, however, operates within current cultural constraining parameters. It is in line with prevailing understandings in many societies, though that is not to claim that it is therefore conservative, or that it is particularly successful in achieving its aim. Moreover, even within those

MARX & ENGELS GET HOPELESSLY LOST ON A RAMBLE.

8. The pun on 'nothing to lose but our chains' also conjures up the multiple and indeterminate routes that ideological decontestations can take.

constraints, there are many alternative methods of redistribution –
recall the many conceptions of the concept of equality.

We conclude that meaning is culturally privileged and that, when
ideologies construct their arguments, they draw on an exceptionally
broad range of conventions and symbols, such as value-systems,
religious beliefs, common practices, and scientific and artistic
fashions. In that very important sense, ideologies are always located
in a particular context. Even when they employ the language of
universalism and of abstraction, it refers to understandings that
emanate from particular societies at a specific historical time. The
notion of universal human rights is a Western cultural notion,
developed over the past 400 years or so, that attempts to occupy the
high ground of a generic claim about human nature and needs. It is
resisted by other cultures for whom differences among humans are
more important than their commonalities, or for whom culturally
justified suffering – at levels unacceptable to most Western
societies – may be inflicted on individuals. However, while cultural
constraints may trump logical ones, by blocking off some
unpalatable logical possibilities, they may also – in the hands of
ideologues – obscure the dictates of logical clarity. The novelty of
the notion of cultural constraints, in the final count, is to advance
the idea of context a little way further than it was taken by earlier
analysts of ideology. Previously, they had seen context as a backdrop
to understanding the genesis of ideological thinking and how it
reflected the social interests of their bearers. Now, context as a
cultural constraint becomes a continuous, living aspect of forming
ideologies, integral to their structure and hence to the messages
they impart.

The four Ps

Having paid attention to the complex conceptual structure of
ideologies, all that remains is to add one final packet of ingredients
to the morphological brew. That refers to the four Ps of
ideological composition: proximity, priority, permeability, and

proportionality. The feature of *proximity* indicates, as we saw above, that political concepts make no sense on their own. They can only be understood when examined within a particular idea-environment of surrounding concepts. If individuality is proximate to an atomistic conception of human nature, a conception that sees the individual as largely self-sufficient, it will play a different role in the given ideology than it would have were individuality to be proximate to a highly sociable conception of human nature. In the first case it will entail political arrangements that secure an optimal private sphere for individuals; whereas in the second it will recognize the importance of social interaction in order to develop one's individuality. Ideologies constitute the necessary space in which political concepts take concrete shape.

The feature of *priority* indicates that the meaning of every political concept in an ideology, as well as of the general arguments of that ideology, is dependent on which concepts (and which conception of each concept) are allocated core significance and which are relegated to the periphery of the ideology. Ideologies experience continuous shifting of the units of furniture within their 'rooms'. A unit may be a centrepiece and be moved later to the side of the room, or even covered up. In the course of the 19th and early 20th centuries, private property migrated within liberal ideology from a core position in the liberal room to a more marginal one. One of the principal functions of ideologies is to rank the major political concepts. Together these concepts are available as a pool of ideas at the disposal of a society, but each ideology chooses those it wishes to emphasize and then arranges the selection in a pecking order. The result is to offer a menu for public consumption through which political decisions may be taken.

Ranking results in a structure of sorts. When we suggest that, to begin with, all ideologies have cores, these are not immanent features that an ideology would have only ideally and irrespective of experience. Instead, these are the ineliminable key concepts that it is deemed to have in actual political usage. Liberalism contains liberty and progress as core concepts not because this is ordained in some metaphysical outreach, but because that is a conclusion we arrive at by listening systematically to liberals and their critics, and by reading the texts they have written. By analogy, kitchens are not invariably products of a cosmic logic. They are convenient spaces that have developed over time in order to satisfy a basic need – food preparation. By common convention, itself a cultural elaboration of basic needs – and not by natural law – kitchens have cookers and sinks. Those are core units, a minimum kit, without which a kitchen would cease to be a kitchen. Likewise, what we have come to call liberalism would no longer be liberalism if it did not place liberty and progress at the core of its concerns – a necessary if not sufficient minimum for sustaining what has become known as liberalism. If this argument is circular, it is simply replicating the circular logic of a language game. But it also reflects sustained empirical, historical usage.

Surrounding the core are adjacent and peripheral concepts. Adjacent concepts flesh out the core. They restrict its capacity for multiple interpretations and pull it in a more defined direction (for liberalism, an adjacent concept might be democracy, as a way of guaranteeing liberty and progress). Peripheral concepts or ideas are more specific and detailed. Most are still significant to the central meanings carried by the ideology, though some may be marginal (for liberalism, a significant peripheral concept might be opposition to censorship, while an increasingly marginal one might be the right to inherit social status). Most of them are situated on the perimeter of an ideology, between thought and action. That is the point where concepts lose their abstraction ('liberty') and are interwoven with the concrete practices sanctioned or condemned by an ideology ('free entry for refugees into a country'). Peripheral concepts are also historically context-bound and therefore more open to change within the broader framework set by the core concepts. Occasionally, though, changes at the periphery may work through back to the core: the equal rights of women, marginal to 19th-century liberalism, have

9. M. C. Escher's engraving 'Concentric rinds' evokes the complex relationship between the core, adjacent and peripheral concepts characteristic of ideological morphology.

become central to the core liberal concepts of individuality and human rationality. Ideological morphology is neither fixed nor shapeless; it is fluid within the Wittgensteinian family resemblances we summoned up above.

The feature of *permeability* indicates that ideologies are not mutually exclusive in their ideas, concepts, and conceptions. Rather, they intersect with one another at multiple points of contact. On one level, every one of the concepts an ideology hosts carries an assortment of components within itself. The concept of democracy does not stand on its own. It *contains* a conception of equality (at the very least, one person one vote) and a conception of liberty (self-government, emancipation from the rule of others). But those are themselves distinct concepts. Hence democracy cannot be disentangled from other concepts, some of whose conceptions help to constitute the concept of democracy, while others undermine it. Thus, some conceptions of equality of opportunity may erode democratic values, and liberty of sorts can be claimed under a tyranny as well. On another level, components of ideologies also intersect with each other: there is extensive agreement among liberals and conservatives about constitutional liberties, and among liberals and socialists about some state intervention in furthering redistribution. Ideologies are not hermetically sealed: they have porous boundaries and will frequently occupy overlapping space. We can refer to them as holding patterns for political ideas, concepts, and words.

The feature of *proportionality* refers to the relative space within each ideology allotted to a particular theme, or cluster of concepts. In part, this is a question of how an ideology wishes to present its arguments. Most libertarians overemphasize individual liberty at the expense of other liberal values such as sociability, rationality, or progress. For them, the securing for individuals of the freedom to act with as little restriction as possible is the prime end of politics, even if this means that individuals make bad choices that inhibit their own progress and that hinder the rational coordination of the actions of one individual with those of another. Inasmuch as libertarians claim to be members of the liberal family, they expand the liberty theme within a limited ideological space in a manner that analysts of liberalism might judge to be disproportionate, while the other themes are squeezed into a small area.

In part this is a question of the best order of magnification for making an impact on the population towards whom the ideology is targeted. What do the authors and disseminators of an ideology want to achieve? Clearly, maximum impact and penetration with respect to their intended consumers. If their arguments are too detailed and complex, they will attract only professional political theorists and philosophers, but be useless as tools of recruitment under an ideological flag. We may focus on a few pixels in detail yet have no idea of the photograph within which they are situated. If the arguments are too general, like a shot of planet earth from the moon, this may satisfy the undiscerning and those alienated from politics, but be ineffectual as a guide for proceeding on specific policy routes. Too much information is as worthless as too little, as we observed when discussing ideologies as maps. Simplification, and occasionally more dangerously oversimplification, is what ideologies do best.

That is not a derogatory conclusion: political systems cannot function without the middle-range magnification that ideologies supply. Political arguments cannot be directed solely at geniuses or experts if they are supposed – as are ideologies – to be tools for the mobilization of collective action. The vast majority of people will experience overload as a consequence of undue complexity: they need information that fits their absorption capabilities in a given field (though they are often led up the garden path by ideologues). Understanding and analysing are acutely reliant on selecting evidence, on establishing artificial order within the disjointed experience of reality that we have. These inevitable processes of selectivity are themselves related to the perceptual and conceptual frameworks we adopt. Ideologies are not exact representations of an ideational reality, but symbolic reconstructions of it. They are based on a collation of fragmented facts and competing values that themselves intervene in that reality. The map often becomes the reality itself.

We have come a long way from the end-of-ideology approach. Consider now how absurd it would be if we announced that concepts would no longer be contestable, that political conceptions cannot combine in myriad ways, that there is no possibility of allocating different levels of importance to a political value, in one scheme propelling it towards the core of our concerns, in another marginalizing the same value. All these consequences would, however, ensue from the end of ideology! Conversely, we have moved away from mechanical and stationary models of ideology – those of pure domination, class interest, and obfuscation – to an appreciation of ideological flexibility. Precisely that flexibility, of which the early discussants of ideology knew little, makes ideologies vehicles of political thought that are particularly suited to accommodate, transmit, and adapt actual political thinking. It also enables students of ideologies to account for the centrality and ubiquity of ideology. Finally, it offers a tool of immense importance to social scientists – a scheme for the complex comparative analysis of ideologies. Ideologies can no longer be distinguished on the basis of the *presence* or *absence* of certain concepts or ideas; instead, the basis of comparison relates to their *location* and *morphology*, to the four Ps. True, that is not the sole basis of comparison, as we shall see below. But it is the one of principal interest to political theorists accustomed to dealing with political concepts, arguments, and texts.

Chapter 5
Thinking about politics: the new boys on the block

Ideology is a mode of thinking about politics. But, saying that, we have to bear two things in mind. First, it is not the only mode. There is a great difference between declaring that *everything* is ideological (as a classical Marxist would have to say of an alienated society) and maintaining that all forms of political thinking have an ideological *dimension* (which is the claim here). Second, morphological analysis is only one means of accessing ideological meaning. The student of ideology needs to be equipped with more than one methodological tool in order to elicit optimal information from ideologies and project on to them a more refined understanding.

Separate but equal agendas?

The great colonizer of the high ground of thinking about politics is political philosophy. Political philosophy brings to the study of political theory an overriding concern with either or both of the following: the moral rightness of the prescriptions it contains, and the logical validity and argumentative coherence of the political philosophy in question. From its known beginnings in classical Greece, political philosophers have been preoccupied with constructing good answers – that is, morally proper and intellectually persuasive answers – to questions such as 'What is justice?' or 'Why should one obey the state?' Increasingly, over the past 400 years or so, they have also concentrated on the minutiae of a good political argument: its rationality, its capacity to identify conceptual distinctions and logical paths of reasoning, whether deductive or inductive, and its internal consistency. Good or bad? Right or wrong? Valid or invalid? Those are the questions that political philosophers pose with respect to the issues they discuss. In so doing, they are expected to engage in reflexive and self-critical thought-processes.

Many philosophers are guided in their enterprise by a notion of truth, at least as an ultimate possibility to be extracted after a difficult process of critical searching and debating. And many of them tend therefore to scoff at the 'truths' of ideologies – as acts of decontestation and closure of debate that are frequently hasty, irresponsible, confused, or even perverted. Philosophers typically assert that ideological thinking is poor-quality thinking that does not merit serious scholarly examination. Whatever else they are, philosophers are professional thinkers whose aim it is to control the quality and subtlety of the arguments they pursue, and who value the argumentative expertise of the individual philosopher of high aptitude.

That is not to contend that philosophers aren't also ideologists. They are. But they do not see themselves primarily as ideologists; their ideologies often accompany them as a surplus of meaning and intention. Thus, philosophers have produced theories of social contract designed to solve *ethical* issues of political trust (the protection of natural rights in return for obeying a government), to respect the natural *rationality* of all people (their preference for peace over war or anarchy), and to present such a contract as the only *logical* possibility for self-preservation. Yet, the ideological baggage they surreptitiously or unconsciously carry includes several features of the ideology known as classical liberalism: a preference for regarding individuals as the prime political actors, the belief that formal equality is sufficient for constructing just political arrangements, and an assumption that human relationships are exchange relationships – because social contracts are modelled on rules of the market.

Ideologies, too, wish to offer arguments that are persuasive, but they go about their business rather differently. Some of them seek to emulate the techniques of political philosophers, but only up to the point where ideological messages will be comprehensible to intelligent citizens untrained in philosophical method. Liberalism and socialism are such ideologies, addressing the critically aware in a society, and proffering ideas meant to convince rationally. Other ideologies may be vaguer in what they offer, whether because their producers haven't thought their arguments through properly, or because the elusiveness discussed above serves them well. 'Watch my lips. No more taxes!', uttered George Bush Senior famously in the 1988 US Presidential elections. This ideological position concerning the freezing of current patterns of redistribution was designed to appeal to almost all people of property in its sweeping generality; however, it proved impossible to sustain. Ideologies, to be sure, need to attract the interest of large political groups; philosophies do not. Philosophers need first and foremost to satisfy their professional colleagues. The test of their success is the rational persuasion of their targeted audience: other philosophers. If their theories find a wider audience, that is indeed a bonus, but the price will necessarily be the vulgarization of their ideas. Transmitters of ideologies need first and foremost to muster significant groups that will assist them in their endeavour to capture control over political language and collective decision-making. That is the test of *their* success.

The ideological promotion of debate depends on an elaborate mixture of rational and non-rational argument. Ideologies of the left and the right have always been especially good at that. They have underpinned their reasonable arguments by calling up emotional terms ranging from solidarity, fraternity, and visions of plenty, through patriotism, honour, and defence of the land, to fear, revenge, and hostility towards others. Invoking the emotions is a highly useful short-cut for ideologies; it is an efficient and undemanding way of obtaining a response. The spread of passion through a group can be swift, and it may have a longer shelf-life. Witness the power of national struggles over language or land that invoke the strongest reactions. Witness also the power of religious fanaticism as a tool of ideological and political dispute. And witness the constant use of rhetoric, even among moderate politicians, as a means for whipping up support or denigrating opposing points of view. 'Give me liberty or give me death', 'back to basics', 'workers of the world, unite' are some examples. I shall return to this theme in Chapter 9.

In short, we need to appreciate that an ideology is a rather different intellectual venture than a political philosophy. It is, above all, a political tool situated firmly within the political domain. Its generators and publicizers have a far keener sense of the political than do most political philosophers. Ideologies are not models of what political thinking should be – a characteristic of political philosophies, especially of the Anglo-American variety – but embrace the patterns of political thinking actually produced by social groups for the consumption of social groups. Ideologies must therefore be judged on a host of criteria. Are they relevant to their temporal and spatial contexts? That must be measured by the degree to which they relate to the vital issues a society confronts and whether their solutions are regarded as workable by significant groups. Are they capable of having an impact on the direction a political system will take? That relates to the degree to which they command respect, wield authority, and permeate decision-making circles. Are they efficient in recruiting devotees and advocates? This relates to the language they employ and whether the messages they send and the manner in which they are conveyed and packaged elicit the desired responses. Are they attractive as doctrine and argument? Most ideologies are sensitive to moral standards, and entertain some aim of bettering social life or at least of protecting its existing values. There are of course exceptions to this among right-wing and totalitarian ideologies, though even they may contain some warped notion of bettering the lives of a few by creating abject misery for others.

Finally, I wish to make an observation not about ideology, but about its students. Studying ideologies is not the same as producing them. It is an attempt to understand and analyse them, just as any student of social and political phenomena would do with respect to his or her area of interest. The first question the student of ideologies needs to pose does not relate to the qualitative substance of the ideology, to its ethical stance or its intellectual weight. It is rather: '*What has to hold* in order for this utterance to make sense/be true/ be right for its producers and consumers?' We have to understand the assumptions contained in an ideology prior to appraising them. We need to put ourselves into the shoes of the ideological promoter, and that requires a sympathetic, or at least impartial, reading of their words and phrases. Were we to direct the full power of philosophical and logical analysis and of ethical evaluation at most ideological material, that material would collapse under the pressure. But instead of concluding that the ideological arguments were hopelessly flawed, we might more wisely decide that we were using the wrong investigative equipment and consequently missing the point.

Nationalism, for example, has been judged by some philosophers to be a mess of shallow and primitive arguments that does not bear serious philosophical scrutiny. This leads to a dead end for anyone who wishes to comprehend the political impact of nationalism as an ideology. Before we proceed any further, we need to know why so many people think it reasonable to privilege their own society above other societies, and why it is that the emotional bond of belonging to a nation acts as a prism through which much political thinking is filtered. More generally, we need to decode the conscious and unconscious presuppositions that enable people to interpret their social worlds and to make factual, or erroneous, statements about those worlds. Only then can we go on to position ideologies at the heart of the political realm, as a form of thought-behaviour that penetrates all political practice. Only then can we ask what purposes ideology serves, and what additional purposes *specific* ideologies serve. And only then can we engage in functional explication.

Conceptual history: harnessing the past

Another tradition of studying political thought has recently emerged under the banner of conceptual history. Conceptual history is a method of investigating the meanings of key political concepts over time, exploring both their accumulative senses and their discontinuities. It is predicated on the assumption that those concepts always reflect their historical contexts, the external events and practices within which ideas take shape. The leading conceptual historian, Reinhart Koselleck, has contended that modern political concepts display increasing abstraction and generality while becoming irreplaceable parts of the political vocabulary. There is now a common acceptance of 'equality' as a desirable key concept, though not of its various conceptions. Conceptual historians emphasize the diachronic (over time) emergence of meaning and its interweaving with synchronic (at a point in time) constructions. To illustrate: our synchronic, current notion of rights as individual claims is nourished by a diachronic evolution of individualism leading to a greater insistence on respect for persons, and by a desire to obtain protection from tyranny (rather than, say, inspired by feudal hierarchies of rights). In turn it redefines our understandings of past rights, so that we no longer tend to explain them as natural and hence discoverable, but as social and hence invented or evolving.

Theories of conceptual history have borrowed insights from linguistics, and the end-result is the identification of a semantic field in which time and space both confer meaning on political language. That perspective differs sharply from the timeless universalization of concepts practised by some political philosophers and from the ahistoricity of many linguists, but it draws heavily on the hermeneutic tradition which, like conceptual history, originated principally in Germany. Conceptual historians acknowledge the importance of social conflict involved in determining the 'correct' meaning of concepts. Political parties, groups, and interests ordinarily contest, or resist the contestation of, the basic concepts. To some, democracy may signal intensified popular participation and control, and to others the rhythmic accountability of political elites at election times. The public interest may conjure up clean air, a national health service, and the transparency of legislation, or it may be used to refer to defence, the governmental shielding of information, and the banning of strikes.

Clearly, a strong affinity obtains between the contemporary study of ideologies and conceptual history. Variability, conflict, context, and the existence of fields of meaning are features held in common. Conceptual historians, obviously, concentrate on change over time. In particular, Koselleck has proposed the idea of shifting horizons of meaning. The meanings of concepts depend on the fusion of past and present horizons, or perspectives. For example, the persistent reference of 19th-century liberal ideologists to past Greek ideals of democracy infused 19th-century views with notions of the nobility of democracy and free speech. In parallel the 19th-century suspicion of the quality of rule that could emanate from the uneducated masses caused its intellectuals to superimpose a representative democracy on the direct democracy inherited from Greece. The representative model, however, was heavily qualified by restricting the vote to those who had an economic stake in the system, and by preferring the governing class to be trained in certain skills. The future is also subject to the projection of expectations nourished in past and present experience. Collective memory is both accumulative and serves as the basis from which to launch future visions. Thus celebrations of the millennium were shaped by past Christian religious experience and by an inherited method of time-keeping that endows round numbers with ceremonial significance. But it was also a statement of expectations of a new beginning, grounded on 19th- and 20th-century hopes for infinitely self-propelling social and technological progress.

Conceptual historians are less fastidious about the sources they use than are philosophers. The classical texts beloved by political philosophers are only one of their concerns, and they are quite happy to peruse newspapers, pamphlets, speeches, party manifestos, and official publications. This move away from elitist articulations is close to the heart of students of ideologies, who share with conceptual historians the common purpose of comprehending ordinary political speech and thought. This quest for the commonplace and the widespread indicates the important step of normalizing ideologies instead of pathologizing them. It brings ideologies into the ambit of the phenomena one would expect to explore when conducting standard political research.

Conceptual historians have reminded us that time is a crucial dimension for studying concepts (and by extension ideologies). Historians of ideas have done this for a while, but one weakness of their past approach has been to abstract the history of a concept from its context. The history of freedom has all too frequently been presented as if one could trace its evolving meanings from ancient times to the present and rest content with that. The historian Quentin Skinner and others have corrected that view through directing historical research towards the intentions of actors and authors, for which an appreciation of the contexts and discontinuities of ideas is essential. When applied to ideologies, time becomes an interactive factor not only in locating but in constituting them. Time, we now know, is not the remorseless ticking of clocks, but can be bent to the human will and subjected to the human imagination. Various conceptions of time animate different ideological tendencies, as the list illustrates in rough terms.

Ideology	Time
reactionary	static (a particular point in time is adhered to)
traditional	repetitive (continual cycles of time)
enlightened-conservative	accumulative (past experience is built on)
classic liberal	incremental (human will produces small changes)
social democratic	evolutionary (a constant improvement over time)
revolutionary	teleological (change is determined by an end-state)
fascist	renewable (a new dawn is breaking)
utopian	projected (unattainable or mythical future time)

Social and historical time does rely on some indisputable facts, but one central feature of ideologies is to link both diachronic and synchronic facts selectively in a web of resourceful imagination. The disjointed becomes joined up; the random becomes open-ended and progressive, or closed and oppressive. Conceptual history and the study of ideologies are cognizant of human agency in choosing our futures, but they are aware of the manifold constraints within which such choices operate. One dictum of Marx's has re-acquired a resonance that analysts of ideology would do well to heed:

> Men make their own history, but they do not make it just as they please; they do not make it under circumstances chosen by themselves, but under circumstances directly encountered, given, and transmitted from the past.

Past packaging limits analysts of ideology in interesting ways, and they have to toe a fine line. The notion of family resemblances enables scholars, as we saw above, to refer to a plethora of socialisms held together by this Wittgensteinian device. Because the monolithic view of ideology at the centre of the Marxist approach was challenged by the indeterminate meanings ideologies could carry, a richer and more pluralistic view of their internal variations emerged. On the other hand, we have already stressed that ideologies differed from the more open texts discussed by hermeneutic scholars *because* of their historical formation, and *because* they constituted political traditions. Those traditions constrained the prospect of an infinite number of liberalisms knocking on the door of the family home and claiming membership. Ultimately, the study of ideologies must be grounded on empirical data, because it concerns actual manifestations of collective political thinking.

How do we decide that a particular set of beliefs is part of ideology A rather than ideology B? This calls for a balance between self-definition (liberals are all those who proclaim themselves liberals) and other-definition (liberals are those who some external authority – say, a scholar of liberalism or a politician – declares to be liberal according to some well-defined criteria). Adolf Hitler's claim to be a national socialist then poses a classificatory problem. Is Nazism merely a version of socialism with a nationalist twist? Here self-definition may not be enough. But, rather than simply assert that it isn't socialism, we require an empirical test of self-definitions. We might read, say, a hundred texts that claim to be on socialism. Some family features will then emerge from our readings, and on their basis we can decide whether national socialism resembles those features sufficiently for it to be deemed a member of the socialist family, or whether the name is (deliberately) misleading and Nazism is really a very different kind of ideological animal. Those texts – as conceptual historians recognise – constitute a past field of mutually reinforcing meanings from which we cannot completely escape.

Labeling an ideology 'socialism' itself moulds an identity that constrains the future movement of the encompassed concepts, and acts in the political world as consciousness-shaper and a regulator of political conduct. 'Socialism' becomes an idea-entity that occupies some of the essential space available for the expression of political ideas. 'Socialism stands for . . .' is a common mode of bestowing the illusion of autonomous life on these specific, contingent, yet aspirationally durable, constructs and traditions. The weaving of that imaginative coherence is a major component in parcelling out the realm of the political. Among themselves, the major ideological families both channel the ways in which those ideas are legitimated, understood, and taken seriously, and crowd out other ways of enunciating effective political thought. Access to the meanings of political concepts is then mediated, and significantly rationed, by having to use the gateways provided by extant ideological families – a practice cemented by a tacit appeal to these labelling conventions.

Chapter 6
The clash of the Titans: the macro-ideologies

We leave for a while the various ways of analysing ideologies and move to survey the forms that political ideologies have adopted. Throughout much of the 20th century the prevailing ideologies have been overarching, inclusive networks of ideas that have offered solutions, deliberately or by default, to all the important political issues confronting a society. Those macro-ideologies have sought social and political acclaim and dominance on both national and international levels. In recognizing their centrality we are deferring to the power of tradition and convention as classifiers of ideologies, not forgetting that other classifications could be retrospectively possible. Liberalism, conservatism, socialism, fascism, communism, and other major families, have been virtually reified as political actors in their own right. Indeed, much of the past century can be viewed as a generally vitriolic, and frequently bloody, battleground among them. Far from being marginal epiphenomena, ideologies have shaped the political experience of the modern world.

Most modern ideologies have adopted an institutional garb, in the form of a political movement or party. This is hardly surprising if we recall that ideologies are competitions over providing plans for public policy. Yet it would still be a mistake to assume that conservatism or liberalism are absolutely identical to what Conservative or Liberal parties stand for. Ideologies are rarely formulated by political parties. The function of parties in relation to ideologies is to present them in immediately consumable form and to disseminate them with optimal efficiency. Parties operate at the mass production end of the long ideological production line. Ideologies *emerge* among groups within a party or outside of it. Those groups may consist of intellectuals or skilled rhetoricians, who themselves are frequently articulating more popular or inchoate beliefs or, conversely, watering down complex philosophical positions.

It is common to describe ideologies as ranging from the left to the right in a continuum of beliefs from communism, through socialism, liberalism, and conservatism, to fascism. Recently, attempts have been made to challenge this ordering. Green political thinkers have famously described themselves as neither left nor right, but in front; some versions of fascism have also, but more dubiously, claimed to be neither left nor right; and the 1990s obsession with 'third ways' has proffered a synthesis of a dialectic view of ideological politics. The advantage of these classifications is that an attractive clarity descends on the marketplace of political ideas – a very useful illusion when mustering support. The left–right continuum, however, is itself largely ideological. It serves the purpose of bestowing a moderate or, respectively, radical or even dangerous aura on an ideology; it suggests that to move among ideologies can be a gradual process; and it indicates that ideologies are mutually exclusive and hence offer clear-cut alternative choices.

None of these implications is correct, but we need both micro- and macro-analysis in order to remedy them. The micro-analysis is provided by the morphological approach to ideologies that offers a way of assembling them and exploring their inter- and intra-relationships. The macro-analysis is provided by looking at ideologies as traditions over time and space, whose imagined aspects themselves become part of political reality. The two approaches are complementary: they offer alternative access to

10. Ideologies alter cases.

studying the same thing. Beginning with the conceptual structure, we may apply the notions of decontestation, family resemblances, core, adjacent, and peripheral concepts, and permeable boundaries to some of the main ideological groupings. Most modern ideologies are complex. They cannot be summarized in oversimplified generalizations such as: liberalism is about liberty; conservatism is about preserving the status quo; and so on. They all exhibit a cluster of core concepts, none of which can be maximized without some damage to the others, and consequently to the ideological profile as a whole. As noted above, the proportionality principle teaches us that, if one concept expands to fill up all available space, it will end by crushing the others or subsuming them within its domain.

Liberalism

Liberalism consists of several core concepts, all of which are indispensable to its current manifestations. The supposition that human beings are *rational*; an insistence on *liberty* of thought and, within some limits, of action; a belief in human and social *progress*; the assumption that the *individual* is the prime social unit and a unique choice maker; the postulation of *sociability* and human benevolence as normal; an appeal to the *general interest* rather than to particular loyalties; and *reservations about power* unless it is constrained and made accountable – all these are the minimum liberal kit. Superimposed on that kit is a crucial disposition: a *critical questioning* of motives and actions that introduces a readiness to rethink one's own conceptual arrangements and practices, and to tolerate those of others.

As a tradition, liberalism entertains the idea of the open-ended development of human beings towards increasingly civilized states of existence, epitomized in John Stuart Mill's writings. That development revolves around the liberty that people can practise unfettered, through not being dominated against their will, abetted by an increasing recognition and formalization of human rights. But throughout the 20th century, the idea of a fair deal to people has grown within the family of liberalisms, consisting not only of equal legal protection and treatment, but the equalizing of economic and gender opportunities and respect for multiple and diverse cultures and faiths within and across nations. Human well-being, or welfare, have come to be principal ingredients of the package of benefits that a humanist political system pledges to its citizens.

Liberalism's achievements have been quietly momentous. Its vision of free peoples bore fruit in the emancipation of colonies from imperial rule. It contributed directly to the liberation of politically marginalized groups from tyranny and discrimination; the very fact that defeated politicians in liberal democracies stand down from power rather than calling in the tanks attests to the assimilation of its norms of political accountability and responsibility. It has promoted social reform on a grand scale, climaxing with the welfare state – witness the legislation for old age pensions, unemployment and health insurance of the Liberal governments in the UK between 1906 and 1914, inspired by the programme of the new liberalism. In international relations the 14 points of American President Woodrow Wilson for the post-First World War settlement envisaged a new world order that initially failed to materialize but that was echoed in the establishing of the United Nations and the Universal Declaration of Human Rights a generation later, and is now slowly spreading to states formerly under totalitarian domination. Every constitution with a bill of rights and a strict demarcation of governmental powers that is honoured by the authorities and the people alike, every system that defers to the rule of law, is a triumph of the liberal tradition. President Roosevelt's 1930s New Deal was one example of liberals acknowledging the need for governments to intervene in order to secure liberty and fairness for their citizens. Another strand of the liberal tradition, to the contrary, has found succour in the advancement of free markets and economic entrepreneurship – shielded from the suspected bureaucratic inefficiency of the state – as the engines of human welfare.

These are some of the more notable milestones of the liberal tradition that have changed the world more than the most dramatic of political revolutions, and have lasted far longer. The liberal tradition has also faltered notably in a number of instances: the weakness of the Weimar Republic in 1920s Germany failed to prevent the rise of Hitler to power; the masculinist biases of liberals have been slow to extend their objective of emancipation to women; and even liberalism's much valued tolerance has found it difficult to grapple with methods of contemporary terror without descending to the moral level of its enemies, and generates perplexity among liberals when confronted with non-liberal cultures in their own societies. At any given point it is important to realize, contra Gramsci, that there exist more non-hegemonic than hegemonic ideologies.

Socialism

Socialism is another of the major ideological families, and it would be premature to announce its demise quite yet. Its impact on the 20th century and on intersecting ideological families has been considerable. Its core conceptual configuration combines the following. First, it sees the *group* as the basic social unit, whether society as a whole or a smaller group such as a commune or a syndicate. For socialists, human beings are constituted by their relationships with their human and, at one remove, their non-human environments. A class, however, is an alienated group, isolated from the material and social goods required for full human development and expression. It therefore has negative connotations, although in several non-Marxist socialisms 'class' has become a *cultural* structure that confers a welcome identity on its members. Second, it has a passion for *equality*, for the removal of hierarchical distinctions, and for the redistribution of goods on the basis of human need. Third, it singles out *work* (also termed labour, creativity, productivity, or activity) as the fundamental constitutive feature of human nature, and accordingly the basic element around which social organization must be structured. Fourth, it cherishes an ideal of human *welfare* or flourishing based in the short run on the elimination of poverty and in the longer run on the free participation of all in the material and intellectual inheritance of humanity. Fifth, it fosters a belief in the promise held out by the *historical process* and the ability of human beings to direct that process to beneficial ends. Socialism is importantly future-oriented and heavily critical of the past and the present. Sometimes in socialist discourse the march of history is unstoppable and the future erupts, erasing all that came before (that is the case with one of socialism's mighty variants, Marxism); at other times it is gradual, erratic, and requires the helping hand of people of good will.

The socialist tradition took off in the late 19th century, prompting European nations in particular to take heed of the demands of the rising working class. Inasmuch as it is justified to refer to an ideological family in the plural, it is certainly justified to talk about socialisms rather than socialism. Several of its versions were messianic and utopian. Socialist anarchists dreamt of the abolition of political power and a spontaneous social order based on altruism and mutual interdependence. Some Marxist-inspired believers went off to found communes like the early kibbutzim over a century ago, in which the family, private property, and the division of labour were abolished in order to create a socially intimate society no longer fractured through barriers of any kind. French and British proto-socialists such as Charles Fourier and Robert Owen designed communities based on radical principles of equality. Syndicalists wished to replace the state with what they saw as the natural political and economic unit: the workplace, following on from identifying work as the essence of being human.

Other socialist versions accepted the institutions of liberal-democracy, but declared their intention to use the state to restructure society gradually, yet inexorably. Among those were members of the Fabian Society in Britain, led by Sidney and Beatrice Webb and George Bernard Shaw, who, punching above

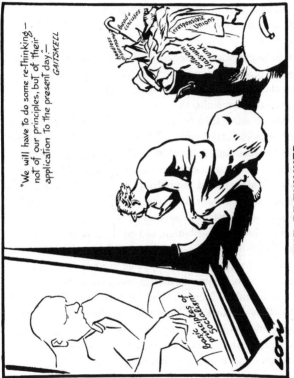

11. The Re-Thinker.

their numerical weight, developed methods of disseminating socialist ideology through cheap and populist publications. They requisitioned the mantle of science through the use of statistics and the breaking down of human beings into measurable categories of neediness: poverty, illness, or enforced idleness. The German socialist Eduard Bernstein was the intellectual leader of their continental equivalents, social democrats heavily committed to an evolutionary path of participatory democracy and increased individual freedom as well as equality.

The immediate political consequence of the socialist tradition was the upsurge of socialist (and in Britain, Labour) parties with a vigorous class agenda. As a consequence, they preferred to concentrate on augmenting the current power of exploited groups rather than investing their faith entirely in the future supersession of prevailing social arrangements. The more effective participation of workers in social and political life, and respect for their rights, became principal socialist ends, promoted by trade unions as well as theorists. Socialism served as a rallying cry of immense potency, as it fostered grand transformative expectations and compelled ruling groups to be on the defensive politically. Nationalization of the means of production, distribution, and exchange became a genuine political objective that was partially realized in the programmes of moderate socialist parties when they came to power in the mid-20th century. More commonly, though, socialists merged with progressive liberal ideologies in developing and consolidating the practices of the welfare state. Here is an apposite example of the intricate relationship between party and ideology. Though socialist parties claimed to have brought the welfare state into the world, it was clearly a liberal construct, balancing public and private responsibility for individual well-being and blending consumer choice with state regulation. Socialist parties provided the muscle for what was originally a liberal ideological scheme, and most of the ideologists of the welfare state were hybrid social-liberals. As we shall see below, all these variants were very different from what became known in Eastern Europe as socialism or communism.

Conservatism

The third major Western ideological family is conservatism. Despite its frequent disclaimers that it isn't an ideology, it too is a particular view of the political world and inevitably contains a series of concepts structured in a specific relationship. The reason why conservatives misread the nature of their belief system, and why adversaries of conservatism have seen it as opportunistic, lies in a peculiar conceptual profile that has disguised its internal consistency. How was it, asked the critics, that conservatives could be paternalist and interventionist in the 19th century, assuming the vocation of protectors and governors of social order, whereas in the late 20th century they aligned themselves with advocates of the free market and minimum state intervention? One historically oriented answer might be that the conservative tradition metamorphosed into something quite different; that it had no fixed substantive position, and merely reflected the policies of the institutions that acted in its name. Accordingly, in Britain the Conservative Party moved from a complacent to a proactive role in the face of industrial strife and the spiralling costs of welfare. On the continent, the Christian Democrats emerged from religiously partisan roots, predominantly Catholic. They then found it heavy going as denominational politics receded in importance, so that conservatives had to realign on the basis of nationalist agendas. That was especially problematic since the continental nationalist tradition had to a considerable extent been taken over by the extreme right, leaving 'normal' conservatives with little space for manœuvre.

But there is another solution to the ostensible elusiveness of conservative ideology. Its critics may have been looking in the wrong place for its core concepts and therefore failed to come up with a durable holding pattern. They have been searching for the conservative counterparts to liberal and socialist ideas concerning human nature, distributive justice, and the relationship between state and individual, and they have drawn a blank. In conservative discourse those ideas do not display a stable continuity and cannot therefore be candidates for core concepts. Yet there *are* such candidates. One common thread running through all conservative argument is an anxiety about change and the urge to distinguish between unnatural and *natural change*. The latter is modelled on continuous organic growth, rather than on disjointed, planned mechanical leaps and bounds. Only change as growth is legitimate, safe, and steady. Another common thread is the conviction that the social order is founded on laws that are insulated from human control; it is therefore impervious to human will, a will that can only tamper with it harmfully. Over time, and as explanatory paradigms of order have altered, different *extra-human origins of a permanent social order* have been invoked: God, nature, history, biology, and economics are some of the more common anchors to which conservatives resort.

Many conservatisms employ religion as a mainstay of the moral and political beliefs they espouse, and use the sanction of religion to impose political order. Indeed, the relationship between the major religions and conservatism is problematic inasmuch as those who hold to their beliefs most strongly, particularly among some Christians, Muslims, and Jews, wish to apply a freeze frame in which the state would become the political instrument of faith. Nature, as already observed, is a favourite ideological artifice for condoning what already exists, or for cloaking the clumsy transparency of social arrangements. History arrives in the form of tradition – appealed to as the cumulative wisdom of the past which the present is fortunate to inherit. Biology and economics are two manifestations of science, whose fashions conservatives engage in their service in order to acquire the status of a secular truth. All these devices deflect criticism away from human beings, especially ruling groups. They can simply disown responsibility for the deficiencies of society, as the latter are apparently ordained by a meta-political framework.

Conservatism is a powerful political tradition because it appeals to human inertia. It also condones the good fortunes of those already in positions of political, economic, and social power, who are understandably reluctant to part with their gains, whether earned, inherited, or acquired by force. Fear is thus a spur to conservatism. Conservative theorizing has also not unduly troubled its supporters. It has not required the great intellectual and imaginative effort that all progressive and reforming ideologies demand: to conjure up a world better than the existing one. Its technique has been largely reactive, and that in two ways. First, although its ideology is normally dormant, it awakens when confronted by the principles and policies of opposing ideologies. Confrontation is built into conservatism, whenever it is challenged by a project it regards both as humanly contrived and breaking with acceptable, organic change. Equality is then matched by natural hierarchy; a developmental individuality by the sobriety of existing cultural norms; a regulatory state by a retreat into civil associations. Revolution is criminalized, utopianism ridiculed.

The second feature of conservative technique is to assemble a counter-set of conceptual configurations, directed against whatever is seen by conservatives as most threatening to the social order. When classical liberals promoted political emancipation in the 19th century, conservatives recalled the duties of the aristocracy and called in the concept of inequality. When socialists pursued social reform and nationalization from the turn of the 19th century and throughout much of the 20th, conservatives hauled property rights to the centre of their ideological room. When fascists employed violence on the streets in the 1930s, conservatives fell back on the rule of law and the constitution. When social democrats advocated planned economies, Thatcherite and Reaganite conservatives applauded the free choice of citizens, deliberately redefined as consumers. Note that in each case these conservative reactions employed concepts and ideas shared with other ideologies (this bears out the point of ideological permeability), but not with the ideology they regarded *at the time* as the most menacing to the core conservative principles. Flexibility in arranging their adjacent concepts helped conservatives to protect their core notions of safe change and the need to shield the social order from the vagaries of the human will. What seemed to its castigators an opportunistic ideology was in fact a highly consistent one. Even the ostensibly radical social transformation engaged in by Thatcherites was intended to re-establish the kind of natural organic change that, in their view, had been undermined by over-generous welfare measures and by trade union politics.

While conservatism was engaged in a psychological as well as a political struggle with the ideologies of moderate and planned reform – liberalism and socialism – the latter two were also at loggerheads with each other. Their relative proximity triggered off the hostility of two groups competing over a similar clientele, forced as a consequence to caricature the differences between them. True, Marxist versions of socialism and libertarian versions of liberalism shared little common ground, but the main body of the two families overlapped on issues of democracy, constitutionalism, and the recognition of the plight of the disadvantaged. Nevertheless, liberals depicted socialism as bureaucratic and unrealistic; socialists retaliated by damning liberalism with endorsing an instrumental egoism that most liberals had already discarded. None of this, however, could match the mortal combat between two newcomers, fascism and communism, and the rest of the ideological field in the middle third of the 20th century. If anything, the emergence of these totalitarian ideologies reinforced the widespread view of ideology as doctrinaire, dogmatic, closed, and inflicted on an unwilling populace.

The totalitarian ideologies

The Italian fascist dictator, Benito Mussolini, employed the notion 'totalitarian' favourably, as indicating a breadth and sweep of social concern and political unity. More commonly, *totalitarianism* was understood as the main feature of an ideology that left no stone unturned in penetrating human activity and even thought. It collapsed the space between the public and private spheres, insisting that the state was entitled to regulate all areas of social and individual life. Hannah Arendt saw it as breaking down the distinction between legality and illegality, so that ordinary citizens never knew on which side of the law they were, a law changed at the whim of the rulers. That itself perpetuated a state of terror and disorientation, through which compliance was extracted from the body politic. Fascism combined a fierce and *aggressive nationalism* at the disposal of the state and its henchmen, a cult of the *leader* (Il Duce), *terror* and physical violence, and a *myth of regeneration* that resurrected the past glories of Rome and promised national rebirth. The German variant, national socialism, was more methodical both in its ideology and its practical realization. It added to the above a *racial myth*, to be achieved by the unification of the pure Aryan race under a thousand-year German Reich, paralleled by the *demonization of Jews* as subhuman and the subsequent mass annihilation of millions. This abstraction from real Jews, to which the myth bore no resemblance, was an ideological contrivance necessary to hold together the disparate and incoherent features of a preposterous doctrine with catastrophic consequences. Leader worship for Der Führer was, if anything, more pronounced than in Italy.

Communism, on the other hand, was a more elusive ideology. For a long while it played on its ideational derivation from the socialist family and from the linguistic interchangeability between socialism and communism as the ideal society held out by Marxists. Instead, it became a perverted offshoot of the socialist tradition. (That usage of 'socialism' was happily accepted by anti-socialists in the West, though not by social-democrats.) Its *elitist* and *totalitarian* features emerged in the Soviet Union under Lenin and, more dramatically, under Stalin, when vast numbers of opponents were murdered in the name of the revolution. After the Second World War, with its spread to Eastern Europe, communism became more bureaucratic and *conservative*. Its discourse still utilized the idea of a *general will*, though no longer a democratic one, represented through the *mass activation* of the people in support of egalitarianism and communal projects. Communist rhetoric was however shorn of its original grand social vision, while retaining *brutal methods of repression* and a systematic abuse of human rights, liberty, and individuality. Communism's most powerful current manifestation, in China, reserved a central guiding role for political elites in fostering a peasant revolution and cultural change, though it is now experimenting with limited free markets.

In the terminology of ideological morphology, the meanings of the concepts used by these totalitarian ideologies, and the proximities among the concepts, were rigidly and inflexibly nailed down. Authority was only associated with the state; the leader with sole knowledge and legitimacy; liberty always meant emancipation from the falsehoods of the other ideologies; and some concepts, such as accountability, rights, and tolerance, were forcibly removed from the political lexicon. This was brilliantly parodied by George Orwell in his novel *Nineteen Eighty-Four*: 'war is peace; freedom is slavery'; 'ignorance is strength'.

As one of its characters put it:

> It's a beautiful thing, the destruction of words . . . Don't you see that the whole aim of Newspeak is to narrow the range of thought? In the end we shall make thought-crime impossible, because there will be no words in which to express it.

Ideology had become, now more than ever, the war of the words. Through it, citizens had a stark choice: they could either find their 'true' political voice or be silenced.

The expansionary ends of Nazism and fascism, as well as their repulsive beliefs and actions, occasioned a world war that, more than most wars, was consciously seen as an ideological struggle to the death between grand systems, dressed up in the dialectical language of good and evil. This epic confrontation was extended to the cold war of the 1950s and 1960s, with communism replacing fascism as the implacable enemy of Western values. The moderate ideologies were encouraged to reject the epithet 'ideology' for themselves, not because they saw ideologies as illusory on the Marxist interpretation, but because – to the contrary – they perceived them as very real and menacing. In retrospect, the dominant mid-20th-century view of ideology was fuelled by the intimate association of ideology with totalitarianism. Through this narrow definition, the defeat of the totalitarian regimes entailed the eradication of ideology itself, and provided ammunition for the 'end of ideology' school. By contrast, current analysts of ideology half a century later are beginning to regard totalitarian ideologies as exceptional rather than normal manifestations of ideology, obscuring the bona-fide ideologies that are far more rooted in social thought and practice.

Chapter 7
Segments and modules: the micro-ideologies

Reshuffling the cards?

It would be wrong to take for granted that the grand ideological traditions, or their virulent counterparts, fill the entire field. Occasionally distinct ideological formations are carved out of an area that straddles two already existing ideologies. In other cases, a full ideological family may act as host to a less developed one. A less developed, or what I shall call thin, ideology, may also exist on its own. Nor should we forget the many non-Western ideological variants that have unjustifiably lived under the shadow of European and North American ideological hegemony. Over the past 25 years, new forms of political thought have emerged in which standard types of political ideologies are not always discernible. Has this changed the nature of ideologies and the way we perceive them?

Any answer must be tentative. On the one hand, we now live in a world loosely described as global, which leads some people to revive the chimera of a universal or global ideology, possibly dominated by icons of American capitalism such as free enterprise and the consumption of Levi jeans, McDonalds hamburgers, Coca Cola, and Microsoft systems. On the other hand, ideologies have been fragmenting into more diverse, unstructured, and temporary combinations that offer partial political solutions while undergoing continuous modification. This slipperiness seems to endorse the ineffectiveness of ideologies at present. Globalization, however, is *not* an ideology but a political and economic process that can denote the breakdown of political borders and of the realm of states; or the spread of certain production and consumption practices across the world; or a demand that claims for justice be treated irrespective of their geographical origin. It may be stimulated by ideological standpoints that originated within liberalism, but it is a misrepresentation and narrowing of the versatility of the liberal tradition.

The revival of free-market, or neo-, liberalism has, after all, recently appeared under a conservative protective mantle. It has also characterized libertarianism, which has broken away from liberalism. Libertarianism affords a typical example of a gravitational shift within conventional ideologies that obscures an ideology's foundational principles by reorganizing the core units of furniture. In this case liberty is associated with unlimited consumer choice while crowding out or demoting other liberal core concepts. The fact that libertarianism is also carved out of conservatism releases a strange hybrid. It includes the sanctioning of existing economic inequalities and a built-in reluctance to contemplate state regulation as a possible cure to social evils. And it frequently takes shelter under the umbrella term 'community', in which a communal *market* supplants the alternative association of community with affective ties of trust and social solidarity.

Perhaps rather than assume the fragmentation of ideologies we should argue that they constituted illusory wholes to begin with. What has changed is not so much the modular structure of ideologies as the public perception that they are being dismantled and reassembled at a rapid rate. The 'third way' is one such example. An amalgamation of social-democratic, conservative, and liberal principles has been packaged and distributed as a new 'ideology' or political programme. The third way – presumably between liberal-capitalism and state-socialism – has combined a liberal belief in rights with a conservative/socialist belief in responsibilities. It has commercialized those rights as privileges to be purchased through responsible behaviour. It has advocated a mixed economy, with the balance being increasingly tilted to the side of private regulation and initiatives. It has endeavoured to moralize citizens and encourage the expression of their plural individualities while creating a powerful centralized and paternalist state. It has preached the primacy of welfare while making it partly conditional upon work (a conservative or socialist value, as you wish). It has sought to modernize relentlessly while relying on traditional family values. This unstable mix may be ephemeral, but it is being kept together by elite governmental manipulation and publicity.

But such top-heavy, artificial ideological compounds are constantly jeopardized by the proliferation of new sources of ideological creativity, assisted by the mass media. Ideological mini-structures may focus around pressure groups, such as anti-immigration campaigners who retreat into a conservative nationalism. They may centre around newspaper crusades, say for the legalization of mild drugs, which relate to issues of liberty and individual lifestyles. And they may be located around popular feeling arising from momentous or disturbing events, such as an earthquake, which brings into play questions of mutual responsibility and the distribution of scarce goods to the needy; or an act of terror, which reimposes the rigid boundaries between 'us' and 'them' that analysts of ideology periodically query and on which ideological discourse thrives. All these cases contribute to the rich patchwork of ideological thinking at the disposal of a reasonably free community, recalling Gramsci's insight into ideology's multiple origins. But they are also exemplars of constricted ideological expression. They differ principally from the mainstream families in evading the formulation of a broad menu of solutions to major socio-political issues.

Thin ideologies

The break-up of ideologies is itself a matter of some dispute. There are those who see it as the personalization and individuation of ideology, a tribute to the greater liberalization and pluralism of contemporary societies. Still, once we begin to talk of a million ideologies, we abandon common sense, as well as missing out on their political flavour. Even the emergence of new forums of debate and information do not offer a clear-cut conclusion. We are repeatedly told that the internet offers such a revolution in the production of ideologies, enabling voluntary and spontaneous groups to converse with each other so that a discourse emerges. It is of course far too early to see these networks as ideological innovators, since they would need to be more publicly and centrally disseminated if they wished to compete over political language and policies.

Others who speak of ideological fragmentation see that as a reflection of social dislocation and the disintegration of conventional social structures. This view is common among post-Marxists and poststructuralists, of which more in the next chapter, but it is widespread also among those who challenge the uniformly stultifying effects of globalization or even of hegemonic nationalisms. Those challengers applaud the rise of local ideologies, even when they promote single issues, or amalgams of such single issues. The new social movements of the late 20th century are one such example. They encouraged a heady mixture of alternative lifestyles, participatory democracy, ecological responsibility, and equal respect for a multitude of group, gender, and ethnic identities. But fragmentation also makes people more vulnerable to control and manipulation, since horizontal ties among individuals weaken. Observe the enormous growth of surveillance by means of closed circuit television in so-called liberal-democratic societies. The incessant regulation of people's lives through mechanisms of bureaucratic accountability, performance league tables, and the imposition of 'good practice' fortified by threats of legal liability, are other examples. Technology can now deliver invasions of privacy undreamt of by totalitarian ideologies that pose a considerable challenge to liberal and progressive systems.

For students of ideology a new problematic arises. Which analytical tools are the most appropriate for studying ideological segments, as well as for studying the new or reinvigorated ideological families – such as feminism, green political thought, and nationalism – that do not claim to be catch-all receptacles with an all-inclusive agenda? Well, segments and modules are not ideologies. A table and chair in an otherwise empty room would be a pitiful semblance of a furnished room indeed. Rather, it conjures up the image of a prison: a room with a constrained and constraining purpose. None the less, minimalist furniture can offer very striking arrangements and highlight a few aesthetic and functional messages, as would an interest group with a singular ideological aim. We are left with two interpretative options. The first is to explore the extent to which ideological modules are actually contained in broader host ideologies, despite their bid for ideational independence. The second is to announce the existence of a new morphological variety, namely, a thin ideology.

A thin ideology is one that, like mainstream ideologies, has an identifiable morphology but, unlike mainstream ideologies, a restricted one. It severs itself from wider ideational contexts by deliberately removing or replacing many concepts we would expect an ideology to include. It does not embrace the full range of questions that the macro-ideologies do, and is limited in its ambitions and scope. Take nationalism, an ideology that concentrates on the *exceptional worth of a nation* as the shaper of human identity while often emphasizing its *superiority* over other national entities, and that justifies the demands a nation can make on the conduct of its members. The point is that is does little else. It certainly does not produce a scheme for the just distribution of scarce and vital goods – the famous 'who gets what, when, how' question that is seen to be central to politics. While it constantly talks up national self-determination, or emancipation from external rule when the nation in question is not governed by an independent state, it is silent on individual liberty and rights and on the desired relations between the public and private spheres.

Nationalism in fact rarely appears in this raw and thin form, unless a specific ethnic group is demanding a nation-state of its own against a hostile political system (for example, the struggle of the Basques against Spain), or an existing nation-state is being threatened by an external enemy threatening to swamp it (for example, the British bulldog image during the Second World War). It is far more likely to be found sheltering within broader host ideologies. Conservatives are happy to find space in their room for the nationalist love affair with an invented history and an exclusive territory. Fascists, of course, exploit nationalism as the justification of offensive militarism directed at real and imagined enemies. This comes with a very physical and racial view of what constitutes the fibre of a nation. Even liberals have periodically come to terms with nationalism, a word they have also shied away from frequently. After all, it sanctions the principle of self-government, and it can be tweaked to advocate the universal right of all nations to possess their own state.

But there is a different take on thin ideologies, as can be seen from the case of feminism. Feminists regard the issue of *gender* as the crucial ingredient of ideological contestation, and the presence of *patriarchal power relationships* as potent a divide as class conflict was for Marxists. They make us face yet again the question of boundaries: what *are* the major ideological groupings, and what *are* the central features of the map that best covers the terrain of ideologies? Whereas many 20th century feminists have regarded their arguments as extensions of liberal or socialist principles, radical feminists argue that the existing array of political concepts and issues often deflects our attention from what really matters. Underlying 'innocuous' uses of the phrase 'human rights' are men's rights. Political power is better understood as patriarchal power.

The dichotomies universal/particular, culture/nature, mind/body, reason/emotion all too frequently mirror those of male/female, with the first of each pair a desirable feature and the second a disorder or pathology. A reordering of political language, and through it of social practices, is the aim of that feminism. Thus what seems a thin ideology from the perspective of conventional ideological analysis may be interpreted as an attempt by feminists to cut the cake differently. On their account, thick ideologies should contain, at least in part, a different set of concepts, including care, nurturing, empathy, and altruism. The ideological struggle over the control of language is not just that of competing over the meanings of prevalent political concepts such as liberty and justice, but one that endeavours to endow concepts customarily held to be apolitical with political import. Throw away much of the existing masculinist map, proclaim radical feminists, and re-explore the territory.

Are ideologies 'Western'?

The fracturing and reordering of ideologies has shaken up the ideological scene in another sense. The ideologies under challenge have typically presented themselves as universal. But once that universality is questioned, once universal ideologies are recognized as emanating from a particular cultural area, space suddenly opens up for non-Western ideologies to appear and be noticed. In part this is the triumph of multiculturalism, in part the outcome of a political flexing of muscles of non-Western viewpoints, hitherto made to feel inferior to the 'modern' implications of the West, or deemed to be at a supposedly earlier stage of political and intellectual development. Many Eastern ideologies are curious amalgams of Western theories and of indigenous cultural paradigms. Japanese politics assigns the term liberal to a broadly conservative movement, and mixes traditionalist norms with hi-tech lifestyles. Technology introduces Western notions of markets, while regional cultures constrain against the Western-type individualism that would normally accompany them.

The rise of religious fundamentalism poses a particularly interesting conundrum for students of ideology. Are religions also ideologies? Do ideologies and religions share common characteristics? After, all, communism has been described as a secular religion – it was even the subject of a famous book called *The God that Failed*. The answer to these questions is unsurprisingly both yes and no. Religions only become political ideologies when they compete over the control of public policy and attempt to influence the social arrangements of the entire political community. Even then, that is a necessary but not sufficient condition for considering them to be ideologies. A religion may serve as a powerful pressure group for the public observance of a day of rest. That does not make it an ideology, not even a thin one, but a single-issue group focusing on one ideological segment – in this case a defining religious and ethical custom of a culture it wishes to preserve. Religious fundamentalism can equally manifest itself in a retreat from the world, or in a utopian messianism that awaits salvation in an unspecified future.

Nevertheless, religious fundamentalism may be heavily politicized and, conversely, *it* can adopt some of the characteristics of totalitarian ideologies. One of these is an expansionist and aggressive attitude towards non-believers, who must either be converted or dispatched. Another is a shared morphological characteristic, namely, a striking inflexibility attached to the meanings of its conceptual clusters. Whereas secular totalitarians lock in the meanings of their concepts through arbitrary linguistic force, religious fundamentalists achieve the same end through their sacred texts. Their holy men assume the role of the guardians and purveyors of the truth, a role that intellectuals occasionally take on – with less authority – in secular ideologies. But in both cases the guardians may be stage-managed from within their midst by people indistinguishable from political dictators.

For the analyst of ideology the real problem of whether religions are ideologies is a question of differentiation. Political Islam, for example, possesses the functions of an ideology in that it provides a collective political agenda, while maintaining a substantial overlap, even identity, between religion and politics. However, it does not possess the *specificity* of contemporary ideologies – distinct, reified, systems of ideas that exist as quasi-autonomous features of our world and can be studied independently. Since the 19th century, the major political ideologies have evolved to become systems of ideas detached from our religious beliefs – just as our ideas about art and about economics now display a considerable degree of autonomy – even though Western political thought itself used to be much more heavily interfused with religious convictions. The modern 'Western' attribute of idea-systems is their crystallization as separate specializations in thought and thought-induced conduct, though dedicated political ideologies and other inclusive thought-systems still exchange mutual influence. Religious fundamentalism, however, provides no space for a political ideology to emerge as a distinct set of ideas from under the wings of religion, nor for a range of religious interpretations to escape from the vice of political discipline. This evident absence of a boundary, in this case between a political ideology and a different kind of belief-system, means that the choice over what to believe in is more limited. You have to embrace larger packages without the option to 'mix and match', to aggregate and disentangle.

The age of the mainstream ideologies is not over. They will no doubt mutate into different variants that surround their core ideas – and they would ossify if they did not – but the constant tidal pull between the decentralization of political power and its recentralization will afford room for novel configurations, while the quickening speed of communication will result in a faster tempo of change. What is clear is that ideologies cannot come to an end, nor is there a winning ideology as announced by the 'end of history' prophets of the 1990s. For that to happen history would have to have a finishing post, and human imagination would have to grind to a halt.

Chapter 8
Discursive realities and surrealities

The general impression of ideological fragmentation and malleability has led to new developments in the theory of ideology. Some scholars are more inclined to study the fragments, while others have reactivated the old Marxist scepticism about what lies behind these continual ideological permutations and what, if anything, is visible when we burrow under them.

Discourse theory

The equivalent of the focus on micro-ideologies is the minute examination of the usages to which language generally, and political language in particular, are put. The branch of studies that sheds light on this is discourse analysis, nourished on the standpoints of hermeneutics, semantics, and postmodern studies. The central idea behind discourse analysis is to conceive of language as a communicative set of interactions, through which social and cultural beliefs and understandings are shaped and circulated. Like previous approaches I have examined, discourse analysis is holistic in its purview, attempting to delineate a total field of communication. Some of it is simply content analysis – an endeavour to explore systematically the patterns of ordinary speech. Other strands are preoccupied with the broader cultural messages exchanged in a discourse, involving assumptions about gender, ethnicity, or power and how these assumptions influence people's lives. Several strands go even further and also regard institutional practices as discourse.

This connects discourse analysis to questions of identity that have come to predominate the academic agenda of several social scientists. How do societies perceive themselves (for example, are they proud and self-congratulatory of their achievements or disillusioned and demoralized)? Which attributes of a society are brought into prominence through the use of narratives that tell us how we came collectively to be what we are (for example, is it our resourcefulness at times of crisis or our devotion to established political rituals)? How are distinctions between 'us' and 'them' fashioned (for instance, do territorial borders delimit the society, or is skin colour an effective divide)? Which linguistic and metaphorical devices are exploited to accentuate deliberately, or to form unconsciously, images and self-understandings of a discursive community (for instance, 'the big apple'; 'better red than dead', 'a green and pleasant land')? As social and political groupings change more rapidly in the contemporary world, the fragility and ephemerality of discourse become more evident. A plethora of discourses, seemingly ever more pliable and alterable, is replacing the past dominant discourses of the Enlightenment or of Christianity. In a rather more hesitant process, even masculinity and hierarchical ethnicities are challenged, and consequently retreat or are reshuffled.

Much discourse theory has developed a *critical* edge that takes us back to Marxist theories of ideology. Discourses become then just the latest way of portraying ideology's pernicious effects – linguistic frameworks in which individuals and groups are trapped, in which communication serves the purpose of concealment and deceit, in which repression and antagonism breed and are perpetuated, and in which one's utterances and texts are mistakenly assumed to be authentic expressions of one's own ideas, rather than implanted from outside. Even seemingly less harmful discourses are exposed for what they really are:

contingent norms of conduct and of thought, masquerading as normal and even universal rules of human interaction. Discourse is transformed from an innocuous fact of social life to a contrivance that permeates human existence by means of the cultural constraints it imposes. As Michel Foucault phrased it, discourse is power, thus extending the sociological insight through which Marx had viewed ideology.

Identity, however, has come to supplant class as the arena in which group destinies are moulded. The struggle over the control of one's identity, resisting the imposition by others of a flawed or irrelevant identity, pervades social power relationships. Meena regards herself primarily as a biochemist, others define her as a Hindu. Robert delights in being a voluntary community worker, others perceive first and foremost a black male. While the aim of discourse analysts is to reveal the nature of the encumbrances that such communication generates, occasionally in great technical detail, the theoretical stance behind that aim can occasionally verge on the nihilistic. Language is seen as the container of infinite possibilities, and there is no fixed archimedal point to direct us towards truth, correctness, or knowledge. *Any* description of Meena is restrictive and misleading of what she is. Change and flux, not fixity, become the new order. When this approach is pushed to its limits, language becomes the only reality. Reality is simply what a discourse ordains reality to be, a discursive construct, and objectivity is a chimerical pursuit even for the scholar.

Ideology and discourse

What of this is relevant to theorizing about ideology? For those who see both discourse and ideology as primarily about power relations, discourses are the communicative practices through which ideology is exercised. For those who see language as the medium through which the world obtains meaning, discourse may replace, or partially depoliticize, the concept of ideology. But we may reformulate that relationship: ideology is one form of discourse but it is not entirely containable in the idea of discourse. To begin with, discourse analysts abandon the representation of reality and plump conclusively for the construction of reality. Ideologies engage in both. They interact with historical and political events and retain some representative value. But they do so while emphasizing some features of that reality and de-emphasizing others, and by adding mythical and imaginary happenings to make up for the 'reality gaps'. A constant feedback operates between the 'soft' ideological imagination and the 'hard' constraints of the real world.

The complexity of analysing a discourse can be illustrated by taking the famous passage from the American Declaration of Independence of 1776:

> We hold these truths to be self-evident, that all men are created equal, that they are endowed by their Creator with certain unalienable Rights, that among these are Life, Liberty and the pursuit of Happiness.

A political philosopher might read this as a complex statement encompassing a number of philosophical assertions:

(1) the *universality* of certain fundamental human attributes;
(2) the extra-human *sanctification* of several essential goods;
(3) faith in the overriding power of *truth*;
(4) the similar *comparative status* of human beings;
(5) the bestowing of entitlements on *individuals*.

It is an account of how things are – political philosophers might call these moral facts – but also an indication of the concrete practices that will result from this view of the world.

A critical discourse analyst may give the passage a rather different reading:

12. The American Declaration of Independence.

(1) It constructs a human identity that *refuses to recognize differences*, while signalling that anyone who does *not accept the truths* of the passage places himself or herself beyond the pale of humanity.

(2) It is a manifestation of *power* inasmuch as it serves the aims of the founders of the USA and implicitly justifies mobilizing the use of force in the name of their ideals, while explicitly shaping human beings in a preferred image.

(3) It attains these ends by using *linguistic strategies* such as the inclusive 'we' and the capitalization of key words.

(4) It tells a story, a brief *narrative*, about how we came to be what we are from the moment of our birth, and it is phrased in vocabulary that an 18th-century American reader might find congenial, and that a contemporary American reader could identify with in broad terms.

(5) It is *gendered*, privileging men.

An analyst of ideology would agree with most of the discourse analysis, but would prefer to examine the more directly political implications of the passage and the intricate micro-structures that reveal specifically ideological decontesting techniques. The work consciously or unconsciously performed by the passage would include:

(1) ruling out certain beliefs from ever being intellectually or rationally challenged, by *protecting* them with the impenetrable and non-transparent shield of self-evidence – as with the emperor's new clothes, only a child or a fool would screw up the courage to query what is presented as inherently obvious and uncontentious;

(2) anchoring political beliefs in powerful *cultural support* systems, in particular an appeal to a divine entity as the shaper and underpinner of the social order;

(3) *prioritizing* a particular set of human characteristics, namely one that maximizes unimpeded and vigorous individual pursuits, that assumes that individuals determine their own fates, and that describes them as possessing unassailable claims to precious social goods;

(4) *advocating* a system of human relations in which human differences are rendered unnatural;

(5) *impressing* the readers of the Declaration with a powerful rhetoric that drives home the significance of its messages, from the smooth confidence generated by a 'declaration' to the staccato enumeration of memorable and easily recognizable rights.

In addition the analyst of ideologies would need to establish the historical roots of the passage, and investigate whether that successful contest over meaning vanquished in its wake all other attempts at decontestation. If so, how does the historical emergence of a dominant ideological variant co-exist with the assertion of discourse analysts that all meaning is a product of language alone? That assertion, central to what has been called the 'linguistic turn', suggests that linguistic polysemy and language games allow infinite possibilities of meaning, so that one meaning cannot conclusively be preferred over another. But does that not let the scholar off too lightly? On the alternative understanding advanced in Chapter 4, I have argued that ideological meaning is located at the meeting place between logical and cultural constraints. In ideological practice, permissible and legitimate meanings restrict the infinity of semantic options that the 'linguistic turn' postulates. In short, ideological meaning is a joint product of the degree of analytical rigour possessed by its formulators, of the linguistic flexibility of language, and of historical context. This may confirm its contingency but not its unlimited content.

Finally, discourse analysts occasionally treat language as a given within which options are barely available to the user caught in the game. The analysis of ideologies, in contrast, pays more respect to the role of individual choice and agency in shifting between disparate interpretations of the world and in refashioning those interpretations, particularly in a society that encourages ideological diversity. It pays more respect to the internal competitions over meaning, as befits a political standpoint. And it pays more respect to the pluralist and manifold nature of differences within an ideological field, while critical discourse theory tends to see the world as dichotomized between notions of the 'self' versus the 'other'.

Post-Marxism: the inevitable elusiveness of reality

Post-Marxists and poststructuralists (sometimes bracketed under the broader label postmodernists) have recently given further impetus to the study of ideologies. Post-Marxists still regard ideology as a means of sustaining collective power, but no longer on the basis of class alone. Poststructuralists are those who challenge the fixity and universality of existing linguistic and political terms and structures. Their method of analysis includes deconstruction – the breaking down of the implicit assumption that language represents reality. They endeavour to expose as misconceived the distinctions and oppositions that language establishes. In part, they follow parallel paths to some of the hermeneutic approaches discussed above, though their expositions are occasionally vitiated by an impenetrable jargon.

Among the more significant writings on ideology to have emerged from these intellectual movements are those of Ernesto Laclau and Chantal Mouffe. Going beyond Althusser's position discussed in Chapter 2, they have disputed the Marxist priority of material base over ideational superstructure as being itself a discursive, rather than a real, relationship. All practices, they argue, are discursive in that they are human, optional, and contingent articulations of how we should understand the world – something entirely different from a claim about what the world is. The social order isn't given; it is constructed or articulated. That produces only the *semblance* of fixity. This argument shies away from the notion of fragmented ideologies, for fragmentation entails the dissolution of a prior whole. Instead, wholes are themselves merely one, precarious, articulation out of an indeterminate number of potential combinations of ideas. Contingency in this case has no opposite (its opposite being necessity), because there is nothing necessary *in* discourse. However, there is something necessary *about* discourse – it is one of the central features of being human. That crucial factor prevents the perceived world from being meaningless or random to its viewers, although students of ideology will always challenge the permanence or absoluteness of the articulated, hegemonic, discourse.

In line with Marxist concerns, post-Marxists associate the analysis of ideology with the large issue of what 'society' itself is, and with the parallel question of the identity of the individual or the 'subject'. In particular, theorists such as Laclau and Mouffe have argued that the elusiveness of what we call 'society' requires the coinage of signifiers, representative words, to paper over the cracks and to invent stability and system where no such things exist. These they term a special category of signifier – 'empty signifiers' that do not represent an external reality but the absence of it. Thus when demonstrators march for 'freedom' it is far from clear what that would entail. Freedom here signifies something that societies cannot ever achieve in full, but the clarion cry 'freedom' produces the illusion that it exists and that a social order based on freedom is attainable. The awful truth that all societies are unfree has to be disguised.

That fanciful production of social order, according to post-Marxists, is the role of ideology. Because a free society is a chimera, ideologies are a necessary illusion. They cannot, contra Marx, wither away, without – as Slavoj Žižek has observed – creating the chaos and panic that staring into the void will cause. Ideology, nevertheless, is in a state of continuous renewal, as new signifiers need to be invented to keep up the masking process when old ones lose their bite. But the secret that has now been let out of the bag is that, in effect, there is nothing behind the mask. Žižek draws on French Lacanian psychoanalytical theory to contend that the horror of contemplating the unknowable leads people to weave imaginary webs, or fantasies, of what they claim can be known, and to fabricate harmonies where antagonisms reign. The dichotomy between the self and the other acquires a spectral, ghostly, status, because the 'other' is a mirage and the 'self' or the subject a temporary identity cobbled together for reasons of psychological comfort, bereft of the capacity for agency with which liberals endow the individual. On views such as these, ideologies cannot even be illusions or distortions. How can one distort truth if there *is* no truth, if reality pure and simple is inaccessible and even unimaginable? How can we know reality when what *we* perceive as reality is something else, filtered through a mesh of symbols? However, if there is no truth, there can be no falsehood (= the corruption of truth). Instead of condemning ideology as false, it should be recognized as a powerful indicator of the ways in which people actually construe the world. It is a fact, we might say, that ideology (wrongly) presents discourse as objective fact. But because discourse is so ephemeral, ideology, according to Žižek, can never properly construct the stability that social life lacks.

In a broader sense, post-Marxists and poststructuralists use ideology as an abstract technical term. It has itself become a signifier with no clear meaning. Its purpose is importantly to warn scholars that they are now entering an area in which their critical faculties have to be engaged (not, as with Marx, an area to be abolished). But ideology retains its negative Marxist connotations; it is the obfuscated way in which reality is presented to all, and it forces people to inhabit a world of constricted structures, or of psychological necessity, from which escape routes are badly marked and usually culs-de-sac. A new generation of critics of ideology has been born, but they have little to offer in return for their discovery of its bleak function. No utopias, no solutions, only the awareness that we move from one make-believe world to another and that, perhaps, we can at least aim for the make-believe that does not fundamentally dehumanize those who hold it. This resistance to empiricism, to sense-evidence other than the evidence of language itself, makes poststructuralism an uneasy partner for the projects of most social scientists and historians.

The poststructuralist view of ideology is radical and the view it offers is austere. Its strength lies in its refusal to take any fact, any opinion, any framework, for granted. At the same time, this is a source of weakness among some of its less sophisticated practitioners. The possibilities of discourse in any society are limited, as we have seen, by its own history, and by the cultural constraints that block off some discursive interpretations of the political world and make several of them more challenging and interesting than others. Nor is it the case that all articulated discourses are hegemonic. Several discourses may compete with each other at any point in time or space. That possibility is obscured by the post-Marxist preference for the Marxist convention of referring to ideology in the singular. Of course, that too is a discursive construct that makes us understand ideology in a particular way – something that, one suspects, discourse analysts would be only too happy to concede.

Chapter 9
Stimuli and responses: seeing and feeling ideology

So far I have dealt with ideology as found in written and spoken language, in texts and utterances. We now have to take on board three further themes. First, ideology appears in many non-verbal forms. Second, even as textual discourse, ideology includes metaphors and stories that are not directly decodable as political language. Third, ideology concerns not only the rational and the irrational, the cognitive and the unconscious, but the emotional as well.

Getting the picture

Throughout history ideologies have been transmitted through visual and pictorial forms. Over the past century, more than ever, with the advent of film and television, of the mass production of art and advertising, visual messages have become a striking and efficient way of conveying a political statement, insinuation, or mood. The Romans already knew about the dramatic sense of the visual, so chillingly and forcefully replicated in the Nazi Nuremberg rallies. The symmetrical choreography of the serried ranks, the inflammatory rhetoric of a leader surrounded by giant emblems, the aural impact of the roar of 'Sieg Heils' – all communicated with immediate effect some of the core Nazi ideas: the power of the undifferentiated mass, the relationship of leader to people, the militarization of the national will, the coordination and unison of popular expression. These ideas were absorbed through head and gut simultaneously, and the experience of participating in this massive ritual must have been unforgettable.

Pictures are central to all of the major ideological families – the dove of peace is a liberal internationalist symbol; the socialist movement has privatized the colour red, politically speaking; Soviet communists used posters and statues of giant workers heroically brandishing their implements of toil; and British conservatives capitalized on bulldogs and Winston Churchill's cigar-chomping face when they wished to indicate tenacity and the will to fight and triumph. But visual images, still or moving, may be subtler than that and not directly associated with the main ideological families. London Underground posters of rolling green countryside, international charities' gruesome photographs of people being tortured, architectural structures of public buildings invoking awe or aesthetic interest, the choice of which skin colour to display when pictures of policemen are used for job recruitment, carry political messages as well.

Many visual images may be seen as artistic technologies designed deliberately, or serving unintentionally, to disseminate ideological messages. To be successful in that role they must possess certain features. One is simplicity. If political texts aimed at mass consumption are simplifications – through sound bites and slogans – that is even more the case for most pictorial representation. Icons, signs, and logos are ways of impressing on someone an easily digestible set of meanings. Think of the communist hammer and sickle, combining force with earthy labour. They also need to be salient to the eye, standing out from other information. Think of a flag flying over an embassy, a haven for its nationals in a foreign field. A third feature is memorableness – the length of time in which their impact is retained. The image needs to operate as an anchor and base for a range of repeated associations, reinforcing the ideological message. Think of Lord Kitchener's eyes and finger

13. A Nazi Nuremberg rally.

picking you out from the crowd: 'Your country needs you!' A fourth characteristic is whether it is aesthetically pleasing or disturbing. Anything but blandness will help to lure the attention of the onlooker. Think of the photograph of the little Vietnamese girl fleeing from the napalm bombs. Those who might complain that this is merely packaging rather than content miss the point. Because the mobilization of support is crucial to the function of ideologies, good packaging may break the ice, penetrating the literacy barrier that would deter many people from paying attention to a more detailed text. Finally, stark visual images are useful in triggering primitive emotional reactions – raw responses that get translated into action more quickly, without being distilled through the medium of reflective evaluation.

Visual images have of course been augmented to a high order of magnitude through the development of mass communications. The mass media proffer a degree of penetration inconceivable in the past, and hence enhance the potential for mobilization that ideologies carry. It is no accident that fascist totalitarianism – an ideology that thrived on its permeation of all aspects of social life – found its most efficient form by drawing on the resources of the highly industrialized and bureaucratized Germany. Pictures, films, rituals, even speeches in which the form of delivery outweighs the content (consider Hitler's rhetorical skills in whipping up mass enthusiasm through rhythm and pitch) are the equivalents of fast food: produced in haste, packaged with maximum allure, and consumed with a short-term effect in immediate thrill or awe, but with questionable long-term benefits for one's body. Indeed, the shorter shelf-life of advertisements, commercials, and posters demonstrates that ideologies, like politicians, tend to prefer immediate impact to distant gains. Memorability may frequently be sacrificed for other advantages.

Visual symbols also discourage the two-way flow of debate and modification that occurs, on the morphological view, in ideologies. There is less movement of the kind, noted in Chapter 4, from the

14. A Bolshevik poster celebrating the First of May, 1920.

periphery to the core, which produces much of the internal flux of a supple ideology. Pictures, posters, advertisements are finished end-products. True, a visual representation may excite a strong reaction, positively or negatively, and, of course, a range of varying interpretations. But because its symbolic representation comes in forms that constantly accost our eyes and swamp our vision, unlike texts that we have to seek out deliberately (the exception would be a slogan), the reaction rarely takes the form of trying to alter it directly. We do not get back to the artist and ask for the painting or poster to be redone in the way that we continuously grapple with certain political texts we want to replace or modify – for example, amending a constitution. People have been trained to challenge and alter written and spoken texts far more proficiently than they can argue with images, because linguistic skills are much more important in the public cultures we inhabit, and because ideas are first and foremost transmitted through language. But even the visual arrangement of texts carries messages of its own: the decision which headline should be above the fold on page 1 of a newspaper, and its typeface size and design, indicate the degree of significance readers should attach to what follows underneath it. Nor are visual images the equivalent of ideological systems. They are rather modules, micro-units, or segments that pack a punch by releasing a concentrated message into the systems they inhabit.

A grey area exists between the use of language to convey political arguments and prescriptions, and the use of metaphor, which often works by appealing to imagery from another walk of life ('a melting-pot'; 'the promised land'; 'the father of the nation', 'the corridors of power'). That is matched by the further devices of myth and story. Both are enjoyable ways of consuming ideological viewpoints. They offer attractive and imaginative packages for key social ideas, heavily disguised as forms of verbal entertainment. Alternatively, they may be viewed as defining narratives, lovingly preserved by societies that pass them on from generation to generation as a valued cultural heritage. Machiavelli's recall of Romulus to illustrate the virtues of the Roman republic, the pioneers that trekked across the American continent, the voyages of the Prophet Muhammad, the legends of King Arthur, and the Bible have all been excavated and replicated to serve foundational ideological ends. These texts frequently evoke not ideas in our minds but pictures; they serve as surrogate visual images.

Ideological passions

The evocative nature of imagery and of myth brings us back to the feature I touched on in Chapter 5: the importance of emotion and feelings in ideologies. The study of ideology recognizes that emotions perform a dual role. On an instrumental level they are employed as apparatuses of ideological argument or messaging. On a more profound level, ideologies are the main form of political thought to accept passion and sentiment as legitimate, indeed ineliminable, forms of political expression. Ideologies reflect the fact that socio-political conduct is not wholly or merely rational or calculating, but highly, centrally, and often healthily emotional. Utilitarian and other philosophical schemes that bypass this vital facet of being human, and of interacting with others, are in danger of impoverishing and caricaturing the realm of the political.

Being emotional, and addressing the emotions, are not flawed ways of thinking about politics. True, in their extreme forms they cause collectivities to act as in a frenzy – mob-rule and lynching spring to mind. But giving vent to emotions is not necessarily being irrational. The German sociologist Max Weber famously distinguished between instrumental and value rationality: the first used a means–end rationality as the criterion by which to judge the most cost-effective set of political goals to pursue; the second adhered to a given value at whatever cost it produced. The non-negotiable assumptions we have observed at the basis of any ideology are examples of value rationality. The point however is that they are usually dressed in a protective emotional coating. Even liberals wax lyrical in extolling the virtues of liberty and call for crusades for freedom. Before analytical philosophers neutered the concept of justice, liberals could talk of the 'enduring glow' its passionate pursuit kindled. Terms such as inspiration, certainty of conviction, compassion, sympathy, and the stirring up of the public imagination can all be found in liberal discourses, but liberals all concurrently insist on retaining a critical cool head in assessing and channelling those emotions.

The intensity of emotional attachment to an ideology is another explanation for potentially totalitarian structures. As we have seen, totalitarian ideology is often the result of imposing and locking into place the meaning of political concepts by linguistic and political fiat. But harnessing the passions can have the same effect. The more intensely emotional is one's commitment to an ideology, the more does that emotional intensity replace the need for external linguistic control. And as with totalitarian superimposition of meaning, intense emotional support for an ideology introduces inflexibility, brittleness, and unwillingness to compromise. These in turn make change unlikely and, when change does come, the entire ideological package is liable to disintegrate. Strong, perhaps violent, emotion acts as the cement that prevents the internal mutation of conceptual meaning within a given ideology. We may again call to mind the character of excessive religious faith. But no ideology can hope to succeed if it aims to be purged of emotion, nor can it relate to the complex realities of human behaviour. And no scholarly analysis of political thought can be complete if it does not respect and investigate the emotional life of the members of a society, rather than ignore it.

Chapter 10
Conclusion: why politics can't do without ideology

If discourse, emotion, criticism, culture all intersect with the concept of ideology and claim it for their own, can politics still declare a prior vested interest in the term; in effect, can 'ideology' be employed as shorthand for 'political ideology'? Does it make sense for the concept to be expanded to the extent that its distinguishing marks become blurred as it serves too many masters? The concept of ideology has had a chequered history, and it is still torn between its negative and positive connotations, and between its critical and interpretative analysis. Does it matter, then, if its ambiguity is further increased by dispersing it among a variety of disciplines? We know of course that words have many meanings – that is an insight central to the study of ideology itself. And it is undeniable that ideology is a term borrowed and occasionally annexed by other disciplines. Apart from its critical Marxist and post-Marxist connotations, it is used loosely by historians as synonymous with a system of ideas or an organizing idea, and by literary and cultural students as a critical concept referring to the structures of dominance around almost any idea or theme. Many of these references to the concept of ideology have contributed to its drift away from politics, especially from the type of micro-political analysis explored in Chapters 4 and 5. Only students of politics have so far tapped into most of the facets of ideology. This is certainly not a case of 'to the victor the spoils' but rather, to the highest bidder for the utility of the concept, the privilege of setting the pace of its development and investigating its further potential.

In this book I have endeavoured to reclaim ideology for politics, not only because – inasmuch as ideologies exercise power – they necessarily exist on a political dimension, but because political studies have assigned ideology centrality and have appropriated the term in a particularly revealing manner. The deep complexity of ideology, and the identification of its core characteristics, all direct us to the discipline of politics as its most congenial stamping ground, as the site where it is comprehensively revealed and where its total range of features is engaged. Such methods for identifying its features, however, must remain merely proposals for using the word 'ideology', not the ultimate statement on a concept that is itself essentially contested.

In effect, the study of ideology is most profitably recognized as the study of actual political thought – the concrete thinking *of* political communities and *within* political communities. For anyone interested in the sphere of politics that study is not an optional extra; it focuses on the world of ideas and symbols through which political actors find their way and comprehend their social surroundings. It informs their practices and institutions and it establishes the parameters of their moral prescriptions and expectations. It may or may not be illusory; it may or may not represent something else outside it – but *initially* it doesn't really matter that much if what we want to do is to understand what political thinking is, long before we deconstruct it critically or expose its pretensions. To explore ideologies is to penetrate the heart of politics, and it requires a sympathetic student, not a dismissive or a disillusioned one. Politics is principally concerned with making collective decisions and with the regulation of conflict that both precedes and follows such decisions. Thinking about politics is always thinking defined by, and channelled in, those directions.

Decontestative thinking, and its study – the attempts to forestall argument, and the methods by which that is achieved – are therefore pivotal to *political* theory. Furthermore, because politics is a social activity, so is thinking about politics. It is not an activity external to politics that can *then* be applied to it – an impression given by many philosophers – but is itself *political* thought-behaviour. Nor are ideologies the kind of externalities that some comparative political scientists identify, externalities that intervene from time to time in a world of interests, contingencies, and leadership skills. Rather, ideologies are an inescapable dimension of these components that bestows on them political presence, and without which they cannot be expressed and embodied.

But even if ideology is comfortably located in the realm of the political, how does one respond to the implication of negatively critical theories of ideology that all discourse is ideological? What then isn't ideology? The lack of a differentiated notion of ideology transforms it into an undiscriminating tool. That would be yet another reason to be sceptical about its merits. It is both more fruitful and more accurate to suggest that human discourse has an ideological *dimension* to it, but that it cannot be reduced to that dimension alone. We abide by the hermeneutical insight that there is more than one way of making sense of a text – it may have literary, aesthetic, or ethical worth as well, for example. We must also acknowledge that not all its ideological dimensions are equally significant or intellectually attractive.

By maintaining that ideology relates to politics and to the collective decisions that characterize it, we are not implying that these decisions are unitary. Nor are we suggesting that the poststructural concern with ideological fragmentation necessarily entails ideological disintegration. One of the striking features of modern (and postmodern) social life is its increased differentiation – the thousands of diverse tasks, roles, and developmental paths that people undertake. In ideological terms we are confronted with individuation: the ability of people to choose among sets of ideas is now publicly legitimated by cultures and political organizations sympathetic to personal choice. While we have categorically maintained that it is premature to portray liberalism as the victorious ideology (and it may well be permanently premature, judging by the nature of ideological contestation), we may note a particular feature of liberalism that is amenable to such individuation.

By encouraging variety and originality, liberalism is better suited than other ideologies to hold together a large degree of structural differences and centrifugality. This always takes place within its non-negotiable core premises but these, fortunately for individuated societies, include reasonable tolerance and hence reasonable pluralism. The very liberalism that sustains the possibility of fragmentation also constrains its nihilistic excesses. If ideological dissent is durable, it is so precisely due to a willingness to accept diversity as desirable, and as enriching all the parties to such pluralism. It is also highly probable that the rise of liberalism itself permitted the growth of individuation, so that we are once again presented with the familiar two-way street, or integration, of theory and practice. Our knowledge of the history of liberalism cautiously projects a pattern of similar expectations on to the future. All this is not to extol liberalism but to point out its compatibilities with modernity and postmodernity. By contrast, the liberal-capitalism currently making a bid for 'globalism' is not really an individuated ideology. It allows for consumer choice, but controls it carefully through marketing and thorough entrepreneurial forms of leadership. The result is new types of uniformity, not diversity. It safeguards an ideological position that, in common with so many other non-liberal ideologies, undervalues the maturity of individual citizens, in this case downgraded to the treasured capacity to shop till they drop. Nor does it augment the genuine liberal struggle against the tendency of rulers (political and economic) to direct and manipulate.

What, one may ask, does the study of ideology do for those who insist, as do the normative political philosophers, that political thought is about creating a better society? The posing of such a question is itself telling. Would we ask such a question of anthropology, concerned as it is with observing the behaviour of human beings in cultural contexts? Is *its* aim to create a better society? Possibly indirectly, as is the case with the analysis of ideologies. Good evaluation and the prescription of valuable solutions are conditional upon good observation and, no less, good interpretation. That is why the critical edge of the Marxist approach to ideology is important. On the whole, however, professional languages such as philosophy are not designed to be good transmitters of ideologies, just as ideologies are inadequate transmitters of philosophical arguments. What makes political thinking *ideological* relates to the linguistic need and interpretative imperative to choose among contested meanings of concepts, in order to attain the control over language that renders collective political action possible. That, of course, is a scholarly and technical reason for the inevitability of ideological dissent, and for the parallel artificiality and contingency of ideological decontestation, and it may be defended by analysts of ideology. What is artificial may still be necessary, even if fragile. Contingency itself becomes inescapable. Decontestation, it is true, can elevate one ideology to hegemonic status, and thus run counter to the unavoidable multiplicity of ideological standpoints. But ideological dissent will exist at the very least below the surface, if not in full view of a society. So in order for dissent to be legitimated, and in order for debate to be pluralist, reasonable ideological disagreement has to be accepted as normal and permissible by the public at large.

Ideologies as political resources

If there is necessarily a dimension of political thought that is ideological, why is ideology *central* to the domain of politics? Its central position is a consequence of four of its features, all of which offer further bases for comparing ideologies. First, ideologies are *typical* forms in which political thought is expressed. Politics is all about the attainment of collective goals, the regulation of conflict within a society and among societies. Ideologies are the arrangements of political thought that illuminate the central ideas, overt assumptions, and unstated biases that in turn drive political conduct. And until we respect and comprehend the ubiquitous, important, and everyday political thinking of a society, we will be unable to explain the nature of politics adequately. The typical can never encompass all we need to know, nor must we confuse it with the conventional or allow it to stifle the exceptional, but it offers an indispensable basis for taking the political pulse of a society.

Second, ideologies are *influential* kinds of political thought. They offer decision-making frameworks without which political action cannot occur. We assume, not without justification, that ideologies are instruments of power, from the viewpoint of the rulers; and instruments of enabling and empowering choice, from the viewpoint of members of an open society. Ideologies are, after all, designed to wield influence on mass publics, or at least on key political groupings, in the quest of those publics and groups to steer public policy-making. Influence obviously cannot be confined to the question of who has won the *semantic* battle of decontestation. We also need to take into account the actual take-up of an ideological argument in a society. That means choosing a point in time carefully: sometimes ideologies take decades and even longer, to emerge in force – the 20th-century genre of neo-liberalism, for instance, germinated from the 1940s until it flowered in the 1980s. Ideologies are assumed to have influence because they have practical import, because they are adopted by significant numbers of adherents, and because their ideas have hit a sensitive spot in national and subnational consciousnesses. For similar reasons they are feared and loathed by some as power constructs, as if ideas were too refined to be sullied with the grime of opportunism, graft, and ambition characteristic of the world of politics.

Third, ideologies are instances of *imaginative creativity* and in that role provide the ideational resources and opportunities from which political systems draw. Clearly, ideologies require some modicum of coherence and consistency, and they may gain considerable effectiveness if they also assume moral force. But their shortcomings on all these accounts, while probably vexing logicians and moral philosophers, cannot detract from the input of ideologies as raw, visionary, constructive, experimental, and, yes, occasionally volatile or dangerous, products of the human mind. Ideologies are instances of the vitality achieved by blending intellectual judgement, emotional satisfaction, and even aesthetic appeal, offering a variety of potential options and social futures from which a society can choose. Not least, the configurative capacity of their morphology serves well the power of the imagination ceaselessly to recombine experience and understanding in new shapes.

Fourth, ideologies need to be *communicable*. They must be easily and attractively embraced by mass publics; they must be couched in non-specialist terms; and in open, participatory systems they need to contribute to general debates on political ends. We should also recall that they are to be found in different textual and visual forms. For the scholar of ideology the challenge is to persuade other scholars that non-complex discourse does not rule out complex analysis, and to remind them that even the great books of political philosophy have to await popular 'translation' if they wish to optimize their ideological potential.

Older theories of ideological dogmatism and stasis are now giving way to newer ones of ideological malleability. Not only does that decisive attribute of ideologies shape the present political world, it will mould its future. Coming social and political developments, even taking on board the inevitable unexpected contingencies that catapult it in *this* rather than *that* direction, are overwhelmingly the product of the current technical and intellectual means at a society's disposal. If we want palatable futures, we need to cultivate the possibilities, and curb the perils, contained in the ideologies of the present.

References and further reading

Chapter 1

Antoine Destutt de Tracy's *Éléments d'Idéologie* (Paris, 1804–15) has not been translated into English. On Destutt de Tracy see E. Kennedy, *Destutt de Tracy and the Origins of "Ideology"* (American Philosophical Society, Philadelphia, 1978).

A useful abbreviated edition is Karl Marx and Frederick Engels, *The German Ideology*, ed. C. J. Arthur (Lawrence & Wishart, London, 1974). For selections from Marx's *Capital* (vols. I and III) see D. McLellan, *Karl Marx: Selected Writings* (Oxford University Press, Oxford, 2000).

Chapter 2

Karl Mannheim, *Ideology and Utopia* (Kegan Paul & Co, London, 1936); Antonio Gramsci, *Selections from Prison Notebooks*, ed. Q. Hoare and G. Newell-Smith (Lawrence & Wishart, London, 1971); Louis Althusser, *Essays on Ideology* (Verso, London, 1984).

Chapter 3

The end of ideology thesis appears in D. Bell, *The End of Ideology: On the Exhaustion of Political Ideas in the Fifties* (Collier Books, New York, 1962) and in Edward Shils, 'The End of Ideology?', *Encounter*, vol. 5 (1955), pp. 52–8.

For R. E. Lane's empiricist treatment of ideology see his *Political Ideology: Why the American Common Man Believes What he Does* (The Free Press, New York, 1962).

Clifford Geertz's path-breaking article is reprinted in his *The Interpretation of Cultures* (Fontana, London, 1993). Ludwig Wittgenstein's thoughts on language games and family resemblances are in his *Philosophical Investigations*, 2nd edn (Blackwell, Oxford, 1958).

Chapter 4

For Paul Ricoeur see his *Lectures on Ideology and Utopia* (Columbia University Press, New York, 1986) and *Interpretation Theory: Discourse and the Surplus of Meaning* (Texas Christian University Press, Fort Worth, 1976).

The references to 1940s and 1950s views on liberty relate to Isaiah Berlin, 'Two Concepts of Liberty' in his *Four Essays on Liberty* (Oxford University Press, Oxford, 1969); Karl Popper, *The Open Society and its Enemies* (Routledge & Kegan Paul, London, 1945); and Jacob Talmon, *The Origins of Totalitarian Democracy* (Secker and Warburg, London, 1952).

A central hermeneutic text is by Hans-Georg Gadamer, *Truth and Method* (Sheed and Ward, London, 1979).

The morphological analysis of ideology is developed in M. Freeden, *Ideologies and Political Theory: A Conceptual Approach* (Clarendon Press, Oxford, 1996).

For essential contestability see W.B. Gallie, 'Essentially Contested Concepts', *Proceedings of the Aristotelian Society*, 56 (1955–6), pp. 167–98.

Chapter 5

For the foremost authority on conceptual history, Reinhart Koselleck, see his *Futures Past* (MIT Press, Cambridge, Mass, 1985). The quotation from Marx is from 'The Eighteenth Brumaire of Louis Bonaparte' in McLellan, *Karl Marx: Selected Writings*, p. 329.

Chapter 6

For a more detailed investigation of the core, adjacent and peripheral concepts of liberalism, socialism and conservatism, see Freeden, *Ideologies and Political Theory*. For separate studies of liberalism see G. de Ruggiero, *The History of European Liberalism* (Beacon Press, Boston, 1959) and R. Bellamy, *Liberalism and Modern Society* (Polity Press, Cambridge, 1992); of socialism see A. Wright, *Socialisms* (Oxford University Press, Oxford, 1987) and D. Sassoon, *One Hundred Years of Socialism: The West European Left in the Twentieth Century* (Tauris, London, 1996); and of conservatism see K. Mannheim, *Conservatism* (Routledge & Kegan Paul, London, 1986) and N. O'Sullivan, *Conservatism* (Dent, London, 1975). For fascism see R. Griffin, *The Nature of Fascism* (Routledge, London, 1991) and R. Eatwell, *Fascism: A History* (Vintage, London, 1996). For totalitarianism see H. Arendt, *The Origins of Totalitarianism* (Meridian Books, Cleveland and New York, 1958). For Marxism and communism see L. Kolakowski, *Main Currents of Marxism*, 3 vols. (Oxford University Press, Oxford, 1981).

Chapter 7

On the Third Way see S. White, ed., *New Labour: The Progressive Future?* (Palgrave, Basingstoke, 2001), and M. Freeden, 'The Ideology of New Labour', *Political Quarterly*, vol. 70 (1999), 42–51.

On nationalism see M. Guibernau, *Nationalisms* (Polity Press, Cambridge, 1996) and A. Vincent, *Nationalism and Particularity* (Cambridge University Press, Cambridge, 2002).

On feminism see V. Bryson, *Feminist Political Theory: An Introduction* (Macmillan, London, 1992) and A. Jaggar, *Feminist Politics and Human Nature* (Rowman & Littlefield, Totowa, NJ, 1988).

For political Islam see D. Eickelman and J. Piscatori, *Muslim Politics* (Princeton University Press, Princeton, N.J., 1996). On a secular 'religion' see R. Crossman, ed., *The God that Failed* (Bantam Books, New York, 1954).

Chapter 8

For discourse analysis see T.A. van Dijk, ed., *Discourse as Structure and Process* and *Discourse as Social Interaction* (Sage Publications, London, 1997) and for a concrete example of critical discourse theory see Michel Foucault, *Power/Knowledge*, ed. C. Gordon (Prentice Hall, New York, 1980).

For a valuable collection of articles on the linguistic turn see R. Rorty, ed., *The Linguistic Turn. Recent Essays in Philosophical Method* (University of Chicago Press, Chicago, 1967).

E. Laclau and C. Mouffe, *Hegemony and Social Strategy* (Verso, London, 1985) have produced a central statement of post-Marxist critical discourse theory. S. Žižek's Lacanian approach is represented in his *The Sublime Object of Ideology* (Verso, London, 1989) and in the introduction to his edited *Mapping Ideology* (Verso, London, 1994).

Chapter 9

On the visual impact of ideological propaganda see for example T. Clark, *Art and Propaganda in the Twentieth Century* (Weidenfeld and Nicolson, London, 1997). For Max Weber's distinction between types of rationality see his *Economy and Society*, ed. G. Roth and C. Wittich, vol. I (University of California Press, Berkeley, 1978), pp. 85–6.

* * *

There is now an extensive literature on ideology and its study. D.A. Apter's edited collection, *Ideology and Discontent* (Free Press, New York, 1964) contains many important articles. Explorations of the Marxist approach to ideology include B. Parekh, *Marx's Theory of Ideology* (Croom Helm, London, 1982); J. Torrance, *Karl Marx's Theory*

of Ideas (Cambridge University Press, Cambridge, 1995); and
G. Therborn, *The Ideology of Power and the Power of Ideology* (Verso, London, 1980). J. B. Thompson has written importantly on European continental perspectives on ideology in his *Studies in the Theory of Ideology* (Polity Press, Oxford, 1984). J. M. Balkin's *Cultural Software: A Theory of Ideology* (Yale University Press, New Haven, 1998) is an intriguing attempt to draw parallels between ideology and the formal evolution and dissemination of culture. M. Freeden's *Ideologies and Political Theory: A Conceptual Approach* (Clarendon Press, Oxford, 1996) has been followed by an edited book, *Reassessing Political Ideologies: The Durability of Dissent* (Routledge, London, 2001), that looks back at the 20th century. Other critical examinations of ideology include J. Larrain, *The Concept of Ideology* (Hutchinson, London, 1979); L. S. Feuer, *Ideology and the Ideologists* (Harper & Row, New York, 1975); R. Boudon, *The Analysis of Ideology* (Polity Press, Oxford, 1989), and T. Eagleton, *Ideology: An Introduction* (Verso, London, 1991).

Introductory treatments of specific ideologies include T. Ball and R. Dagger, *Political Ideologies and the Democratic Ideal*, 3rd edn. (Longman, New York, 1999); A. Vincent, *Modern Political Ideologies*, 2nd edn. (Blackwell, Oxford, 1995); R. Eatwell and A. Wright, eds., *Contemporary Political Ideologies*, 2nd edn. (Pinter, London, 1999); R. Eccleshall et al., *Political Ideologies: An Introduction*, 3rd edn., (Routledge, London, 2003); A. Heywood, *Political Ideologies: An Introduction*, 3rd edn. (Palgrave, Basingstoke, 2003).

There is also a specialist periodical, the *Journal of Political Ideologies*, published by Taylor and Francis.

Index

Index

Ideology

Expand your collection of
VERY SHORT INTRODUCTIONS

Visit the
VERY SHORT
INTRODUCTIONS
Web site

www.oup.co.uk/vsi

➤ **Information** about all published titles

➤ News of **forthcoming books**

➤ **Extracts** from the books, including titles
not yet published

➤ **Reviews** and views

➤ **Links** to other **web sites** and main
OUP web page

➤ Information about **VSIs in translation**

➤ **Contact** the editors

➤ **Order** other **VSIs** on-line

LOGIC
A Very Short Introduction
Graham Priest

Logic is often perceived as an esoteric subject, having little to do with the rest of philosophy, and even less to do with real life. In this lively and accessible introduction, Graham Priest shows how wrong this conception is. He explores the philosophical roots of the subject, explaining how modern formal logic deals with issues ranging from the existence of God and the reality of time to paradoxes of self-reference, change, and probability. Along the way, the book explains the basic ideas of formal logic in simple, non-technical terms, as well as the philosophical pressures to which these have responded. This is a book for anyone who has ever been puzzled by a piece of reasoning.

'a delightful and engaging introduction to the basic concepts of logic. Whilst not shirking the problems, Priest always manages to keep his discussion accessible and instructive.'

Adrian Moore, St Hugh's College, Oxford

'an excellent way to whet the appetite for logic. . . . Even if you read no other book on modern logic but this one, you will come away with a deeper and broader grasp of the *raison d'être* for logic.'

Chris Mortensen, University of Adelaide

www.oup.co.uk/isbn/0-19-289320-3

POLITICS
A Very Short Introduction
Kenneth Minogue

In this provocative but balanced essay, Kenneth Minogue discusses the development of politics from the ancient world to the twentieth century. He prompts us to consider why political systems evolve, how politics offers both power and order in our society, whether democracy is always a good thing, and what future politics may have in the twenty-first century.

> 'This is a fascinating book which sketches, in a very short space, one view of the nature of politics … the reader is challenged, provoked and stimulated by Minogue's trenchant views.'
>
> **Ian Davies, *Talking Politics***

> 'a dazzling but unpretentious display of great scholarship and humane reflection'
>
> **Neil O'Sullivan, University of Hull**

www.oup.co.uk/vsi/politics

PHILOSOPHY
A Very Short Introduction
Edward Craig

This lively and engaging book is the ideal introduction for anyone who has ever been puzzled by what philosophy is or what it is for.

Edward Craig argues that philosophy is not an activity from another planet: learning about it is just a matter of broadening and deepening what most of us do already. He shows that philosophy is no mere intellectual pastime: thinkers such as Plato, Buddhist writers, Descartes, Hobbes, Hume, Hegel, Darwin, Mill and de Beauvoir were responding to real needs and events – much of their work shapes our lives today, and many of their concerns are still ours.

'A vigorous and engaging introduction that speaks to the philosopher in everyone.'

John Cottingham, University of Reading

'addresses many of the central philosophical questions in an engaging and thought-provoking style ... Edward Craig is already famous as the editor of the best long work on philosophy (the Routledge Encyclopedia); now he deserves to become even better known as the author of one of the best short ones.'

Nigel Warburton, The Open University

www.oup.co.uk/isbn/0-19-285421-6

INTELLIGENCE
A Very Short Introduction
Ian J. Deary

Ian J. Deary takes readers with no knowledge about the science of human intelligence to a stage where they can make informed judgements about some of the key questions about human mental activities. He discusses different types of intelligence, and what we know about how genes and the environment combine to cause these differences; he addresses their biological basis, and whether intelligence declines or increases as we grow older. He charts the discoveries that psychologists have made about how and why we vary in important aspects of our thinking powers.

'There has been no short, up to date and accurate book on the science of intelligence for many years now. This is that missing book. Deary's informal, story-telling style will engage readers, but it does not in any way compromise the scientific seriousness of the book . . . excellent.'

Linda Gottfredson, University of Delaware

'Ian Deary is a world-class leader in research on intelligence and he has written a world-class introduction to the field . . . This is a marvellous introduction to an exciting area of research.'

Robert Plomin, University of London

www.oup.co.uk/isbn/0-19-289321-1

CONTINENTAL PHILOSOPHY
A Very Short Introduction
Simon Critchley

Continental philosophy is a contested concept which cuts to the heart of the identity of philosophy and its relevance to matters of public concern and personal life. This book attempts to answer the question 'What is Continental philosophy?' by telling a story that began with Kant 200 years ago and includes discussions of major philosophers like Nietzsche, Husserl and Heidegger. At the core of the book is a plea to place philosophy at the centre of cultural life, and thus reawaken its ancient definition of the love of wisdom that makes life worth living.

'Antagonism and mutual misrepresentation between so-called analytical and continental philosophy have helped shape the course of every significant development in Western intellectual life since the 1960s – structuralism, post-structuralism, postmodernism, gender studies, etc. Simon Critchley has skilfully and sympathetically sketched continental lines of thought so that strangers to their detail may enter them systematically enough that their principle texts begin to illuminate one another. It is a remarkable achievement.'

Stanley Cavell, Harvard University

www.oup.co.uk/isbn/0-19-285359-7